MW01285061

# Lord Arthur Saville's Crime

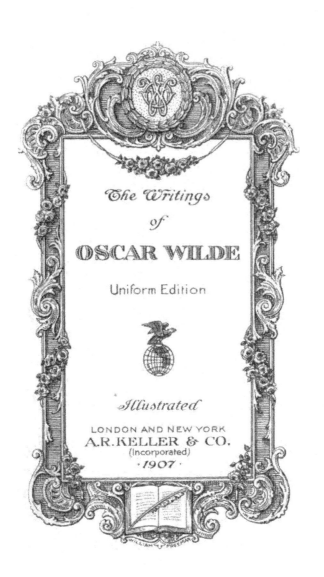

The Writings

of

# OSCAR WILDE

Uniform Edition

Illustrated

LONDON AND NEW YORK
A.R. KELLER & CO.
(Incorporated)
· 1907 ·

*UNIFORM EDITION*

# THE WRITINGS

OF

# OSCAR WILDE

Lord Arthur Savile's Crime
The Portrait of Mr. W. H.
**and**
Other Stories

ILLUSTRATED

London: New York:
A. R. KELLER & CO., Inc.
1907

J. F. Tapley Co.
Printers and Binders
New York

# ILLUSTRATIONS.

# CONTENTS.

# Lord Arthur Savile's Crime.

## A Study of Duty.

# LORD ARTHUR SAVILE'S CRIME.

## I.

It was Lady Windermere's last reception before Easter, and Bentinck House was even more crowded than usual. Six Cabinet Ministers had come on from the Speaker's Levée in their stars and ribands, all the pretty women wore their smartest dresses, and at the end of the picture-gallery stood the Princess Sophia of Carlsrühe, a heavy Tartar-looking lady, with tiny black eyes and wonderful emeralds, talking bad French at the top of her voice, and laughing immoderately at everything that was said to her. It was certainly a wonderful medley of people. Gorgeous peeress chatted affably to violent Radicals, popular preachers brushed coat-tails with eminent sceptics, a perfect bevy of bishops kept following a stout prima-donna from room to room, on the staircase stood several Royal Academicians, disguised as artists, and it was said that at one time the supper-room was abso-

lutely crammed with geniuses. In fact, it was
one of Lady Windermere's best nights, and the
Princess stayed till nearly half-past eleven.

As soon as she had gone, Lady Windermere
returned to the picture-gallery, where a celebrated political economist was solemnly explaining the scientific theory of music to an indignant
virtuoso from Hungary, and began to talk to
the Duchess of Paisley. She looked wonderfully
beautiful with her grand ivory throat, her large
blue forget-me-not eyes, and her heavy coils of
golden hair. *Or pur* they were—not that pale
straw colour that nowadays usurps the gracious
name of gold, but such gold as is woven into
sunbeams or hidden in strange amber; and they
gave to her face something of the frame of a
saint, with not a little of the fascination of a
sinner. She was a curious psychological study.
Early in life she had discovered the important
truth that nothing looks so like innocence as an
indiscretion; and by a series of reckless esca-
pades, half of them quite harmless, she had
acquired all the privileges of a personality. She
had more than once changed her husband;
indeed, Debrett credits her with three marriages;
but as she had never changed her lover, the

world had long ago ceased to talk scandal about
her. She was now forty years of age, childless,
and with that inordinate passion for pleasure
which is the secret of remaining young.

Suddenly she looked eagerly round the room,
and said, in her clear contralto voice, "Where is
my cheiromantist?"

"Your what, Gladys?" exclaimed the Duchess, giving an involuntary start.

"My cheiromantist, Duchess; I can't live
without him at present."

"Dear Gladys! you are always so original,"
murmured the Duchess, trying to remember
what a cheiromantist really was, and hoping it
was not the same as a cheiropodist.

"He comes to see my hand twice a week regu-
larly," continued Lady Windermere, "and is
most interesting about it."

"Good heavens!" said the Duchess to herself,
"he is a sort of cheiropodist after all. How very
dreadful. I hope he is a foreigner at any rate.
It wouldn't be quite so bad then."

"I must certainly introduce him to you."

"Introduce him!" cried the Duchess; "you
don't mean to say he is here?" and she began
looking about for a small tortoise-shell fan and

a very tattered lace shawl, so as to be ready to go at a moment's notice.

"Of course he is here, I would not dream of giving a party without him. He tells me I have a pure psychic hand, and that if my thumb had been the least little bit shorter, I should have been a confirmed pessimist, and gone into a convent."

"Oh, I see!" said the Duchess, feeling very much relieved; "he tells fortunes, I suppose?"

"And misfortunes, too," answered Lady Windermere, "any amount of them. Next year, for instance, I am in great danger, both by land and sea, so I am going to live in a balloon, and draw up my dinner in a basket every evening. It is all written down on my little finger, or on the palm of my hand, I forget which."

"But surely that is tempting Providence, Gladys."

"My dear Duchess, surely Providence can resist temptation by this time. I think every one should have their hands told once a month, so as to know what not to do. Of course, one does it all the same, but it is so pleasant to be warned. Now, if some one doesn't go and fetch Mr. Podgers at once, I shall have to go myself."

"Let me go, Lady Windermere," said a tall handsome young man, who was standing by, listening to the conversation with an amused smile.

"Thanks so much, Lord Arthur; but I am afraid you wouldn't recognise him."

"If he is as wonderful as you say, Lady Windermere, I couldn't well miss him. Tell me what he is like, and I'll bring him to you at once."

"Well, he is not a bit like a cheiromantist. I mean he is not mysterious, or esoteric, or romantic-looking. He is a little, stout man, with a funny, bald head, and great gold-rimmed spectacles; something between a family doctor and a country attorney. I'm really very sorry, but it is not my fault. People are so annoying. All my pianists look exactly like poets, and all my poets look exactly like pianists; and I remember last season asking a most dreadful conspirator to dinner, a man who had blown up ever so many people, and always wore a coat of mail, and carried a dagger up his shirt-sleeve; and do you know that when he came he looked just like a nice clergyman, and cracked jokes all the evening? Of course, he was very amusing,

and all that, but I was awfully disappointed;
and when I asked him about the coat of mail,
he only laughed, and said it was far too cold
to wear in England. Ah, here is Mr. Podgers!
Now, Mr. Podgers, I want you to tell the Duchess
of Paisley's hand. Duchess, you must take
your glove off. No, not the left hand, the other.''

"Dear Gladys, I really don't think it is quite
right," said the Duchess, feebly unbuttoning a
rather soiled kid glove.

"Nothing interesting ever is," said Lady
Windermere: "*on a fait le monde ainsi.* But I
must introduce you. Duchess, this is Mr. Podgers, my pet cheiromantist. Mr. Podgers, this
is the Duchess of Paisley, and if you say that
she has a larger mountain of the moon than I
have, I will never believe in you again."

"I am sure, Gladys, there is nothing of the
kind in my hand," said the Duchess gravely.

"Your Grace is quite right," said Mr. Podgers, glancing at the little fat hand with its short
square fingers, "the mountain of the moon is not
developed. The line of life, however, is excellent. Kindly bend the wrist. Thank you. Three
distinct lines on the *rascette!* You will live to
a great age, Duchess, and be extremely happy.

Ambition—very moderate, line of intellect not exaggerated, line of heart——"

"Now, do be indiscreet, Mr. Podgers," cried Lady Windermere.

"Nothing would give me greater pleasure," said Mr. Podgers, bowing, "if the Duchess ever had been, but I am sorry to say that I see great permanence of affection, combined with a strong sense of duty"

"Pray go on, Mr. Podgers," said the Duchess, looking quite pleased.

"Economy is not the least of your Grace's virtues," continued Mr. Podgers, and Lady Windermere went off into fits of laughter.

"Economy is a very good thing," remarked the Duchess complacently; "when I married Paisley he had eleven castles, and not a single house fit to live in."

"And now he has twelve houses, and not a single castle," cried Lady Windermere.

"Well, my dear," said the Duchess, "I like——"

"Comfort," said Mr. Podgers, "and modern improvements, and hot water laid on in every bedroom. Your Grace is quite right. Comfort is the only thing our civilisation can give us."

"You have told the Duchess's character admirably, Mr. Podgers, and now you must tell Lady Flora's;" and in answer to a nod from the smiling hostess, a tall girl, with sandy Scotch hair, and high shoulder-blades, stepped awkwardly from behind the sofa, and held out a long, bony hand with spatulate fingers.

"Ah, a pianist! see," said Mr. Podgers, "an excellent pianist, but perhaps hardly a musician. Very reserved, very honest, and with a great love of animals."

"Quite true!" exclaimed the Duchess, turning to Lady Windermere, "absolutely true! Flora keeps two dozen collie dogs at Macloskie, and would turn our town house into a menagerie if her father would let her."

"Well, that is just what I do with my house every Thursday evening," cried Lady Windermere, laughing, "only I like lions better than collie dogs."

"Your one mistake, Lady Windermere," said Mr. Podgers, with a pompous bow.

"If a woman can't make her mistakes charming, she is only a female," was the answer. "But you must read some more hands for us. Come, Sir Thomas, show Mr. Podgers yours;"

and a genial-looking old gentleman, in a white waist-coat, came forward, and held out a thick rugged hand, with a very long third finger.

"An adventurous nature; four long voyages in the past, and one to come. Been shipwrecked three times. No, only twice, but in danger of a shipwreck your next journey. A strong Conservative, very punctual, and with a passion for collecting curiosities. Had a severe illness between the ages of sixteen and eighteen. Was left a fortune when about thirty. Great aversion to cats and Radicals."

"Extraordinary!" exclaimed Sir Thomas; "you must really tell my wife's hand, too."

"Your second wife's," said Mr. Podgers quietly, still keeping Sir Thomas's hand in his. "Your second wife's. I shall be charmed;" but Lady Marvel, a melancholy-looking woman, with brown hair and sentimental eyelashes, entirely declined to have her past or her future exposed; and nothing that Lady Windermere could do would induce Monsieur de Koloff, the Russian Ambassador, even to take his gloves off. In fact, many people seemed afraid to face the odd little man with his stereotyped smile, his gold spectacles, and his bright, beady eyes; and when

he told poor Lady Fermor, right out before
every one, that she did not care a bit for music,
but was extremely fond of musicians, it was
generally felt that cheiromancy was a most
dangerous science, and one that ought not to
be encouraged, except in a *tête-a-tête*.

Lord Arthur Savile, however, who did not
know anything about Lady Fermor's unfortunate story, and who had been watching Mr.
Podgers with a great deal of interest, was filled
with an immense curiosity to have his own hand
read, and feeling somewhat shy about putting
himself forward, crossed over the room to where
Lady Windermere was sitting, and, with a
charming blush, asked her if she thought Mr.
Podgers would mind.

"Of course, he won't mind," said Lady Windermere, "that is what he is here for. All my
lions, Lord Arthur, are performing lions, and
jump through hoops whenever I ask them. But
I must warn you beforehand that I shall tell
Sybil everything. She is coming to lunch with
me to-morrow, to talk about bonnets, and if Mr.
Podgers finds out that you have a bad temper,
or a tendency to gout, or a wife living in Bays-

water, I shall certainly let her know all about it.''

Lord Arthur smiled, and shook his head. "I am not afraid," he answered. "Sybil knows me as well as I know her.''

"Ah! I am a little sorry to hear you say that. The proper basis for marriage is a mutual misunderstanding. No, I am not at all cynical, I have merely got experience, which, however, is very much the same thing. Mr. Podgers, Lord Arthur Savile is dying to have his hand read. Don't tell him that he is engaged to one of the most beautiful girls in London, because that appeared in the *Morning Post* a month ago.''

"Dear Lady Windermere," cried the Marchioness of Jedburgh, "do let Mr. Podgers stay here a little longer. He has just told me I should go on the stage, and I am so interested.''

"If he has told you that, Lady Jedburgh, I shall certainly take him away. Come over at once, Mr. Podgers, and read Lord Arthur's hand.''

"Well," said Lady Jedburgh, making a little *moue* as she rose from the sofa, "if I am not to be allowed to go on the stage, I must be allowed to be part of the audience at any rate.''

"Of course; we are all going to be part of the audience," said Lady Windermere; "and now, Mr. Podgers, be sure and tell us something nice. Lord Arthur is one of my special favourites."

But when Mr. Podgers saw Lord Arthur's hand he grew curiously pale, and said nothing. A shudder seemed to pass through him, and his great bushy eyebrows twitched convulsively, in an odd, irritating way they had when he was puzzled. Then some huge beads of perspiration broke out on his yellow forehead, like a poisonous dew, and his fat fingers grew cold and clammy.

Lord Arthur did not fail to notice these strange signs of agitation, and, for the first time in his life, he himself felt fear. His impulse was to rush from the room, but he restrained himself. It was better to know the worst, whatever it was, than to be left in this hideous uncertainty.

"I am waiting, Mr. Podgers," he said.

"We are all waiting," cried Lady Windermere, in her quick, impatient manner, but the cheiromantist made no reply.

"I believe Arthur is going on the stage," said

*'His spectacles seemed almost to touch the palm.'*
Page 15

Of course; we are all going to be part of the
. . ," said Lady Windermere; "and now,
. . s, be sure and tell us something nice.
. . r is one of my special favourites."

. . . n Mr. Podgers saw Lord Arthur's
. . w curiously pale, and said nothing.
. seemed to pass through him, and his
. . . eyebrows twitched convulsively, in
. . . . way they had when he was
. . some h . . beads of perspiration
. . is yellow forehead, like a poison-
. . d his fat fingers grew cold and

. . . . r did not fail to notice these
. . s of agitation, and for the first time
. . himself felt fear. His impulse
. . from the room, but he restrained
. . better to know the worst, what-
. . . . to be left in this hideous uncer-

. . . Mr. Podgers," he said.
. . . ling," cried Lady Winder-
. . impatient manner, but she
. . reply.
. . is going on the stage,' said

Lady Jedburgh, "and that, after your scolding, Mr. Podgers is afraid to tell him so."

Suddenly Mr. Podgers dropped Lord Arthur's right hand, and seized hold of his left, bending down so low to examine it that the gold rims of his spectacles seemed almost to touch the palm. For a moment his face became a white mask of horror, but he soon recovered his *sangfroid*, and looking up at Lady Windermere, said with a forced smile, "It is the hand of a charming young man."

"Of course it is!" answered Lady Windermere, "but will he be a charming husband? That is what I want to know."

"All charming young men are," said Mr. Podgers.

"I don't think a husband should be too fascinating," murmured Lady Jedburgh pensively, "it is so dangerous."

"My dear child, they never are too fascinating," cried Lady Windermere. "But what I want are details. Details are the only things that interest. What is going to happen to Lord Arthur?"

"Well, within the next few months Lord Arthur will go on a voyage——"

"Oh yes, his honeymoon, of course!"

"And lose a relative."

"Not his sister, I hope?" said Lady Jedburgh, in a piteous tone of voice.

"Certainly not his sister," answered Mr. Podgers, with a deprecating wave of the hand, "a distant relative merely."

"Well, I am dreadfully disappointed," said Lady Windermere. "I have absolutely nothing to tell Sybil to-morrow. No one cares about distant relatives nowadays. They went out of fashion years ago. However, I suppose she had better have a black silk by her; it always does for church, you know. And now let us go to supper. They are sure to have eaten everything up, but we may find some hot soup. François used to make excellent soup once, but he is so agitated about politics at present, that I never feel quite certain about him. I do wish General Boulanger would keep quiet. Duchess, I am sure you are tired?"

"Not at all, dear Gladys," answered the Duchess, waddling towards the door. "I have enjoyed myself immensely, and the cheiropodist, I mean the cheiromantist, is most interesting.

Flora, where can my tortoise-shell fan be? Oh, thank you, Sir Thomas, so much. And my lace shawl, Flora? Oh, thank you, Sir Thomas, very kind, I'm sure;" and the worthy creature finally managed to get downstairs without dropping her scent-bottle more than twice.

All this time Lord Arthur Savile had remained standing by the fireplace, with the same feeling of dread over him, the same sickening sense of coming evil. He smiled sadly at his sister, as she swept past him on Lord Plymdale's arm, looking lovely in her pink brocade and pearls, and he hardly heard Lady Windermere when she called to him to follow her. He thought of Sybil Merton, and the idea that anything could come between them made his eyes dim with tears.

Looking at him, one would have said that Nemesis had stolen the shield of Pallas, and shown him the Gorgon's head. He seemed turned to stone, and his face was like marble in its melancholy. He had lived the delicate and luxurious life of a young man of birth and fortune, a life exquisite in its freedom from sordid care, its beautiful boyish insouciance;

and now for the first time he became conscious of the terrible mystery of Destiny, of the awful meaning of Doom.

How mad and monstrous it all seemed! Could it be that written on his hand, in characters that he could not read himself, but that another could decipher, was some fearful secret of sin, some blood-red sign of crime? Was there no escape possible? Were we no better than chessmen, moved by an unseen power, vessels the potter fashions at his fancy, for honour or for shame? His reason revolted against it, and yet he felt that some tragedy was hanging over him, and that he had been suddenly called upon to bear an intolerable burden. Actors are so fortunate. They can choose whether they will appear in tragedy or in comedy, whether they will suffer or make merry, laugh or shed tears. But in real life it is different. Most men and women are forced to perform parts for which they have no qualifications. Our Guildensterns play Hamlet for us, and our Hamlets have to jest like Prince Hal. The world is a stage, but the play is badly cast.

Suddenly Mr. Podgers entered the room. When he saw Lord Arthur he started, and his coarse, fat face became a sort of greenish-yellow colour. The two men's eyes met, and for a moment there was silence.

"The Duchess has left one of her gloves here, Lord Arthur, and has asked me to bring it to her," said Mr. Podgers finally. "Ah, I see it on the sofa! Good evening."

"Mr. Podgers, I must insist on your giving me a straightforward answer to a question I am going to put to you."

"Another time, Lord Arthur, but the Duchess is anxious. I am afraid I must go."

"You shall not go. The Duchess is in no hurry."

"Ladies should not be kept waiting, Lord Arthur," said Mr. Podgers, with his sickly smile. "The fair sex is apt to be impatient."

Lord Arthur's finely-chiselled lips curled in petulant disdain. The poor Duchess seemed to him of very little importance at that moment. He walked across the room to where Mr. Podgers was standing, and held his hand out.

"Tell me what you saw there," he said. "Tell me the truth. I must know it. I am not a child."

Mr. Podgers' eyes blinked behind his gold-rimmed spectacles, and he moved uneasily from one foot to the other, while his fingers played nervously with a flash watch-chain.

"What makes you think that I saw anything in your hand, Lord Arthur, more than I told you?"

"I know you did, and I insist on your telling me what it was. I will pay you. I will give you a cheque for a hundred pounds."

The green eyes flashed for a moment, and then became dull again.

"Guineas?" said Mr. Podgers at last, in a low voice.

"Certainly. I will send you a cheque to-morrow. What is your club?"

"I have no club. That is to say, not just at present. My address is——, but allow me to give you my card;" and producing a bit of gilt-edged pasteboard from his waist-coat pocket, Mr. Podgers handed it, with a low bow, to Lord Arthur, who read on it,

---

*MR. SEPTIMUS R. PODGERS*

*Professional Cheiromantist*

*103a West Moon Street*

---

"My hours are from ten to four," murmured Mr. Podgers mechanically, "and I make a reduction for families."

"Be quick," cried Lord Arthur, looking very pale, and holding his hand out.

Mr. Podgers glanced nervously round, and drew the heavy *portière* across the door.

"It will take a little time, Lord Arthur, you had better sit down."

"Be quick, sir," cried Lord Arthur again, stamping his foot angrily on the polished floor.

Mr. Podgers smiled, drew from his breast-pocket a small magnifying glass, and wiped it carefully with his handkerchief.

"I am quite ready," he said.

## II.

Ten minutes later, with face blanched by terror, and eyes wild with grief, Lord Arthur
Savile rushed from Bentinck House, crushing
his way through the crowd of fur-coated footmen that stood round the large striped awning,
and seeming not to see or hear anything. The
night was bitter cold, and the gas-lamps round
the square flared and flickered in the keen wind;
but his hands were hot with fever, and his forehead burned like fire. On and on he went,
almost with the gait of a drunken man. A policeman looked curiously at him as he passed,
and a beggar, who slouched from an archway
to ask for alms, grew frightened, seeing misery
greater than his own. Once he stopped under
a lamp, and looked at his hands. He thought
he could detect the stain of blood already upon

them, and a faint cry broke from his trembling lips.

Murder! that is what the cheiromantist had seen there. Murder! The very night seemed to know it, and the desolate wind to howl it in his ear. The dark corners of the street were full of it. It grinned at him from the roofs of the houses.

First he came to the Park, whose sombre woodland seemed to fascinate him. He leaned wearily up against the railings, cooling his brow against the wet metal, and listening to the tremulous silence of the trees. "Murder! murder!" he kept repeating, as though iteration could dim the horror of the word. The sound of his own voice made him shudder, yet he almost hoped that Echo might hear him, and wake the slumbering city from its dreams. He felt a mad desire to stop the casual passer-by, and tell him everything.

Then he wandered across Oxford Street into narrow, shameful alleys. Two women with painted faces mocked at him as he went by. From a dark courtyard came a sound of oaths and blows, followed by shrill screams, and, huddled upon a damp door-step, he saw the crook-

backed forms of poverty and eld. A strange
pity came over him. Were these children of sin
and misery predestined to their end, as he to
his? Were they, like him, merely the puppets
of a monstrous show?

And yet it was not the mystery, but the comedy of suffering that struck him; its absolute
uselessness, its grotesque want of meaning.
How incoherent everything seemed! How lack-
ing in all harmony! He was amazed at the dis-
cord between the shallow optimism of the day,
and the real facts of existence. He was still
very young.

After a time he found himself in front of
Marylebone Church. The silent roadway looked
like a long riband of polished silver, flecked here
and there by the dark arabesques of waving
shadows. Far into the distance curved the line
of flickering gas-lamps, and outside a little
walled-in house stood a solitary hansom, the
driver asleep inside. He walked hastily in the
direction of Portland Place, now and then looking round, as though he feared that he was being
followed. At the corner of Rich Street stood
two men, reading a small bill upon a hoarding.
An odd feeling of curiosity stirred him, and he

crossed over. As he came near, the word "Murder," printed in black letters, met his eye. He started, and a deep flush came into his cheek. It was an advertisement offering a reward for any information leading to the arrest of a man of medium height, between thirty and forty years of age, wearing a billy-cock hat, a black coat, and check trousers, and with a scar upon his right cheek. He read it over and over again, and wondered if the wretched man would be caught, and how he had been scarred. Perhaps, some day, his own name might be placarded on the walls of London. Some day, perhaps, a price would be set on his head also.

The thought made him sick with horror. He turned on his heel, and hurried on into the night.

Where he went he hardly knew. He had a dim memory of wandering through a labyrinth of sordid houses, of being lost in a giant web of sombre streets, and it was bright dawn when he found himself at last in Piccadilly Circus. As he strolled home towards Belgrave Square, he met the great waggons on their way to Covent Garden. The white-smocked carters, with their pleasant sun-burned faces and coarse curly hair,

strode sturdily on, cracking their whips, and
calling out now and then to each other; on the
back of a huge grey horse, the leader of a jang-
ling team, sat a chubby boy, with a bunch of
primroses in his battered hat, keeping tight hold
of the mane with his little hands, and laughing;
and the great piles of vegetables looked like
masses of jade against the morning sky, like
masses of green jade against the pink petals of
some marvellous rose.    Lord Arthur felt curiously affected, he could not tell why.    There
was something in the dawn's delicate loveliness
that seemed to him inexpressibly pathetic, and
he thought of all the days that break in beauty,
and that set in storm.    These rustics, too, with
their rough, good-humoured voices, and their
nonchalant ways, what a strange London they
saw!    A London free from the sin of night and
the smoke of day, a pallid, ghost-like city, a desolate town of tombs!    He wondered what they
thought of it, and whether they knew anything
of its splendour and its shame, of its fierce,
fiery-coloured joys, and its horrible hunger, of
all it makes and mars from morn to eve.    Probably it was to them merely a mart where they
brought their fruits to sell, and where they

tarried for a few hours at most, leaving the streets still silent, the houses still asleep. It gave him pleasure to watch them as they went by. Rude as they were, with their heavy, hob-nailed shoes, and their awkward gait, they brought a little of Arcady with them. He felt that they had lived with Nature, and that she had taught them peace. He envied them all that they did not know.

By the time he had reached Belgrave Square the sky was a faint blue, and the birds were be-ginning to twitter in the gardens.

# III.

When Lord Arthur woke it was twelve o'clock
and the mid-day sun was streaming through the
ivory-silk curtains of his room.  He got up and
looked out of the window.  A dim haze of heat
was hanging over the great city, and the roofs of
the houses were like dull silver.  In the flickering green of the square below some children were
flitting about like white butterflies, and the
pavement was crowded with people on their way
to the Park.  Never had life seemed lovelier
to him, never had the things of evil seemed more
remote.

Then his valet brought him a cup of chocolate
on a tray.  After he had drunk it, he drew aside
a heavy *portière* of peach-coloured plush, and
passed into the bathroom.  The light stole softly from above,· through thin slabs of transpar-

ent onyx, and the water in the marble tank glimmered like a moonstone. He plunged hastily in, till the cool ripples touched throat and hair, and then dipped his head right under, as though he would have wiped away the stain of some shameful memory. When he stepped out he felt almost at peace. The exquisite physical conditions of the moment had dominated him, as indeed often happens in the case of very finely-wrought natures, for the senses, like fire, can purify as well as destroy.

After breakfast he flung himself down on a divan, and lit a cigarette. On the mantel-shelf, framed in dainty old brocade, stood a large photograph of Sybil Merton, as he had seen her first at Lady Noel's ball. The small, exquisitely-shaped head drooped slightly to one side, as though the thin, reed-like throat could hardly bear the burden of so much beauty; the lips were slightly parted, and seemed made for sweet music; and all the tender purity of girlhood looked out in wonder from the dreaming eyes. With her soft, clinging dress of *crêpe-de-chine*, and her large leaf-shaped fan, she looked like one of those delicate little figures men find in the olive-woods near Tanagra; and there was a touch of Greek grace in her pose and attitude. Yet she was not *petite*. She was simply perfectly proportioned—a rare thing in an age when so many women are either over life-size or insignificant.

Now as Lord Arthur looked at her, he was filled with the terrible pity that is born of love. He felt that to marry her, with the doom of murder hanging over his head, would be a betrayal like that of Judas, a sin worse than any the Borgia had ever dreamed of. What happiness could there be for them, when at any moment he might be called upon to carry out the awful prophecy written in his hand? What manner of life would be theirs while Fate still held this fearful fortune in the scales? The marriage must be postponed, at all costs. Of this he was quite resolved. Ardently through he loved the girl, and the mere touch of her fingers, when they sat together, made each nerve of his body thrill with exquisite joy, he recognised none the less clearly where his duty lay, and was fully conscious of the fact that he had no right to marry until he had committed the murder. This done, he could stand before the altar with Sybil Merton, and give his life into her hands without terror of wrongdoing. This done, he could take her to his arms, knowing that she would never have to blush for him, never have to hang her head in shame. But done it must be first; and the sooner the better for both.

Many men in his position would have preferred the primrose path of dalliance to the steep heights of duty; but Lord Arthur was too conscientious to set pleasure above principle. There was more than mere passion in his love; and Sybil was to him a symbol of all that is good and noble. For a moment he had a natural repugnance against what he was asked to do, but it soon passed away. His heart told him that it was not a sin, but a sacrifice; his reason reminded him that there was no other course open. He had to choose between living for himself and living for others, and terrible though the task laid upon him undoubtedly was, yet he knew that he must not suffer selfishness to triumph over love. Sooner or later we are all called upon to decide on the same issue—of us all, the same question is asked. To Lord Arthur it came early in life—before his nature had been spoiled by the calculating cynicism of middle-age, or his heart corroded by the shallow, fash-

ionable egotism of our day, and he felt no hesi-
tation about doing his duty.   Fortunately also,
for him, he was no mere dreamer, or idle dilet-
tante.   Had he been so, he would have hesitated, like Hamlet, and let irresolution mar his
purpose.   But he was essentially practical.
Life to him meant action, rather than thought.
He had that rarest of all things, common sense.

The wild, turbid feelings of the previous
night had by this time completely passed away,
and it was almost with a sense of shame that
he looked back upon his mad wanderings from
street to street, his fierce emotional agony.   The
very sincerity of his sufferings made them seem
unreal to him now.   He wondered how he could
have been so foolish as to rant and rave about
the inevitable.   The only question that seemed
to trouble him was, whom to make away with;
for he was not blind to the fact that murder,
like the religions of the Pagan world, requires
a victim as well as a priest.   Not being a genius,
he had no enemies, and indeed he felt that this
was not the time for the gratification of any
personal pique or dislike, the mission in which he
was engaged being one of great and grave solem-
nity.   He accordingly made out a list of his

friends and relatives on a sheet of notepaper, and after careful consideration, decided in favour of Lady Clementina Beauchamp, a dear old lady who lived in Curzon Street, and was his own second cousin by his mother's side. He had always been very fond of Lady Clem, as every one called her, and as he was very wealthy himself, having come into all Lord Rugby's property when he came of age, there was no possibility of his deriving any vulgar monetary advantage by her death. In fact, the more he thought over the matter, the more she seemed to him to be just the right person, and, feeling that any delay would be unfair to Sybil, he determined to make his arrangements at once.

The first thing to be done was, of course, to settle with the cheiromantist; so he sat down at a small Sheraton writing-table that stood near the window, drew a cheque for £105, payable to the order of Mr. Septimus Podgers, and, enclosing it in an envelope, told his valet to take it to West Moon Street. He then telephoned to the stables for his hansom, and dressed to go out. As he was leaving the room, he looked at Sybil Merton's photograph, and swore that, come

what may, he would never let her know what he
was doing for her sake, but would keep the
secret of his self-sacrifice hidden always in his
heart.

On his way to the Buckingham, he stopped at
a florist's, and sent Sybil a beautiful basket of
narcissi, with lovely white petals and staring
pheasants' eyes, and on arriving at the club,
went straight to the library, rang the bell, and
ordered the waiter to bring him a lemon-and-
soda, and a book on Toxicology. He had fully
decided that poison was the best means to adopt
in this troublesome business. Anything like
personal violence was extremely distasteful to
him, and, besides, he was very anxious not to
murder Lady Clementina in any way that might
attract public attention, as he hated the idea of
being lionised at Lady Windermere's, or seeing
his name figuring in the paragraphs of vulgar
society-newspapers. He had also to think of
Sybil's father and mother, who were rather old-
fashioned people, and might possibly object to
the marriage if there was anything like a scandal, though he felt certain that if he told them
the whole facts of the case they would be the
very first to appreciate the motives that had

actuated him.  He had every reason, then, to decide in favour of poison.  It was safe, sure, and quiet, and did away with any necessity for painful scenes, to which, like most Englishmen, he had a rooted objection.

Of the science of poisons, however, he knew absolutely nothing, and as the waiter seemed quite unable to find anything in the library but Ruff's *Guide* and Bailey's *Magazine*, he examined the book-shelves himself, and finally came across a handsomely-bound edition of the *Pharmacopœia*, and a copy of Erskine's *Toxicology*, edited by Sir Mathew Reid, the President of the Royal College of Physicians, and one of the oldest members of the Buckingham, having been elected in mistake for somebody else; a *contretemps* that so enraged the Committee, that when the real man came up they black-balled him unanimously.  Lord Arthur was a good deal puzzled at the technical terms used in both books, and had begun to regret that he had not paid more attention to his classics at Oxford, when in the second volume of Erskine, he found a very interesting and complete account of the properties of aconitine, written in fairly clear English.  It seemed to him to be exactly the poison he wanted. It was swift—indeed, almost immediate, in its effect—perfectly painless, and when taken in the form of a gelatine capsule, the mode recommended by Sir Mathew, not by any means unpalatable. He accordingly made a note, upon his shirt-cuff, of the amount necessary for a fatal dose, put the books back in their places, and strolled up St. James's Street to Pestle and Humbey's, the great chemists. Mr. Pestle, who always attended personally on the aristocracy, was a good deal surprised at the order, and in a very deferential manner murmured something about a medical certificate being necessary. However, as soon as Lord Arthur explained to him that it was for a large Norwegian mastiff that he was obliged to get rid of, as it showed signs of incipient rabies, and had already bitten the coachman twice in the calf of the leg, he expressed himself as being perfectly satisfied, complimented Lord Arthur on his wonderful knowledge of Toxicology, and had the prescription made up immediately.

Lord Arthur put the capsule into a pretty little silver *bonbonnière* that he saw in a shop-window in Bond Street, threw away Pestle and

Humbey's ugly pill-box, and drove off at once to Lady Clementina's.

"Well, *monsieur le mauvais sujet*," cried the old lady, as he entered the room, "why haven't you been to see me all this time?"

"My dear Lady Clem, I never have a moment to myself," said Lord Arthur, smiling.

"I suppose you mean that you go about all day long with Miss Sybil Merton, buying *chiffons* and talking nonsense? I cannot understand why people make such a fuss about being married. In my day we never dreamed of billing and cooing in public, or in private for that matter."

I assure you I have not seen Sybil for twenty-four hours, Lady Clem. As far as I can make out, she belongs entirely to her milliners."

"Of course; that is the only reason you come to see an ugly old woman like myself. I wonder you men don't take warning. *On a fait des folies pour moi*, and here I am, a poor, rheumatic creature, with a false front and a bad temper. Why, if it were not for dear Lady Jansen, who sends me all the worst French novels she can find, I don't think I could get through the day. Doctors are no use at all, except to get fees out of one.   They can't even cure my heart-burn."

"I have brought you a cure for that, Lady Clem," said Lord Arthur gravely.   "It is a wonderful thing, invented by an American."

"I don't think I like American inventions, Arthur.   I am quite sure I don't.   I read some American novels lately, and they were quite nonsensical."

"Oh, but there is no nonsense at all about this, Lady Clem!   I assure you it is a perfect cure.   You must promise to try it;" and Lord Arthur brought the little box out of his pocket, and handed it to her.

"Well, the box is charming, Arthur.   Is it really a present?   That is very sweet of you. And is this the wonderful medicine?   It looks like a *bonbon*.   I'll take it at once."

"Good heavens! Lady Clem," cried Lord Arthur, catching hold of her hand, "you mustn't do anything of the kind.   It is a homœopathic medicine, and if you take it without having heart-burn, it might do you no end of harm. Wait till you have an attack, and take it then. You will be astonished at the result."

"I should like to take it now," said Lady

Clementina, holding up to the light the little transparent capsule, with its floating bubble of liquid aconitine. "I am sure it is delicious. The fact is that, though I hate doctors, I love medicines. However, I'll keep it till my next attack."

"And when will that be?" asked Lord Arthur eagerly. "Will it be soon?"

"I hope not for a week. I had a very bad time yesterday morning with it. But one never knows."

"You are sure to have one before the end of the month then, Lady Clem?"

"I am afraid so. But how sympathetic you are to-day, Arthur! Really, Sybil has done you a great deal of good. And now you must run away, for I am dining with some very dull people, who won't talk scandal, and I know that if I don't get my sleep now I shall never be able to keep awake during dinner. Good-bye, Arthur, give my love to Sybil, and thank you so much for the American medicine."

"You won't forget to take it, Lady Clem, will you?" said Lord Arthur, rising from his seat.

"Of course I won't, you silly boy. I think it

is most kind of you to think of me, and I shall write and tell you if I want any more."

Lord Arthur left the house in high spirits, and with a feeling of immense relief.

That night he had an interview with Sybil Merton. He told her how he had been suddenly placed in a position of terrible difficulty, from which neither honour nor duty would allow him to recede. He told her that the marriage must be put off for the present, as until he had got rid of his fearful entanglements, he was not a free man. He implored her to trust him, and not to have any doubts about the future. Everything would come right, but patience was necessary.

The scene took place in the conservatory of Mr. Merton's house, in Park Lane, where Lord Arthur had dined as usual. Sybil had never seemed more happy, and for a moment Lord Arthur had been tempted to play the coward's part, to write to Lady Clementina for the pill, and to let the marriage go on as if there was no such person as Mr. Podgers in the world. His better nature, however, soon asserted itself, and even when Sybil flung herself weeping into his arms, he did not falter. The beauty that stirred his senses had touched his conscience also. He felt that to wreck so fair a life for the sake of a few months' pleasure would be a wrong thing to do.

He stayed with Sybil till nearly midnight, comforting her and being comforted in turn, and early the next morning he left for Venice, after writing a manly, firm letter to Mr. Merton about the necessary postponement of the marriage.

## IV.

In Venice he met his brother, Lord Surbiton,
who happened to have come over from Corfu in
his yacht. The two young men spent a delightful fortnight together. In the morning they
rode on the Lido, or glided up and down the
green canals in their long black gondola; in the
afternoon they usually entertained visitors on
the yacht; and in the evening they dined at
Florian's, and smoked innumerable cigarettes
on the Piazza. Yet somehow Lord Arthur was
not happy. Every day he studied the obituary
column in the *Times*, expecting to see a notice
of Lady Clementina's death, but every day he
was disappointed. He began to be afraid that
some accident had happened to her, and often
regretted that he had prevented her taking the
aconitine when she had been so anxious to try
its effect. Sybil's letters, too, though full of

love, and trust, and tenderness, were often very sad in their tone, and sometimes he used to think that he was parted from her for ever.

After a fortnight Lord Surbiton got bored with Venice, and determined to run down the coast to Ravenna, as he heard that there was some capital cock-shooting in the Pinetum. Lord Arthur, at first, absolutely refused to come, but Surbiton, of whom he was extremely fond, finally persuaded him that if he stayed at Danielli's by himself he would be moped to death, and on the morning of the 15th they started, with a strong nor'-east wind blowing, and a rather sloppy sea. The sport was excellent, and the free, open-air life brought the colour back to Lord Arthur's cheeks, but about the 22d he became anxious about Lady Clementina, and, in spite of Surbiton's remonstrances, came back to Venice by train.

As he stepped out of his gondola on to the hotel steps, the proprietor came forward to meet him with a sheaf of telegrams. Lord Arthur snatched them out of his hand, and tore them open. Everything had been successful. Lady Clementina had died quite suddenly on the night of the 17th!

His first thought was for Sybil, and he sent
her off a telegram announcing his immediate
return to London.  He then ordered his valet
to pack his things for the night mail, sent his
gondoliers about five times their proper fare,
and ran up to his sitting-room with a light step
and a buoyant heart.  There he found three letters waiting for him.  One was from Sybil herself, full of sympathy and condolence.  The
others were from his mother, and from Lady
Clementina's solicitor.  It seemed that the old
lady had dined with the Duchess that very
night, had delighted every one by her wit and
*esprit,* but had gone home somewhat early, com-
plaining of heartburn.  In the morning she was
found dead in her bed, having apparently suffered no pain.  Sir Mathew Reid had been sent
for at once, but, of course, there was nothing to
be done, and she was to be buried on the 22d at
Beauchamp Chalcote.  A few days before she
died she had made her will, and left Lord Arthur her little house in Curzon Street, and all
her furniture, personal effects, and pictures,
with the exception of her collection of minia-
tures, which was to go to her sister, Lady Margaret Rufford, and her amethyst necklace, which

Sybil Merton was to have. The property was not of much value; but Mr. Mansfield the solicitor was extremely anxious for Lord Arthur to return at once, if possible, as there were a great many bills to be paid, and Lady Clementina had never kept any regular accounts.

Lord Arthur was very much touched by Lady Clementina's kind remembrance of him, and felt that Mr. Podgers had a great deal to answer for. His love of Sybil, however, dominated every other emotion, and the consciousness that he had done his duty gave him peace and comfort. When he arrived at Charing Cross, he felt perfectly happy.

The Mertons received him very kindly, Sybil made him promise that he would never again allow anything to come between them, and the marriage was fixed for the 7th of June. Life seemed to him once more bright and beautiful, and all his old gladness came back to him again.

One day, however, as he was going over the house in Curzon Street, in company with Lady Clementina's solicitor and Sybil herself, burning packages of faded letters, and turning out drawers of odd rubbish, the young girl suddenly gave a little cry of delight.

"What have you found, Sybil?" said Lord Arthur, looking up from his work, and smiling.

"This lovely little silver *bonbonnière*, Arthur. Isn't it quaint and Dutch? Do give it to me! I know amethysts won't become me till I am over eighty."

It was the box that had held the aconitine.

Lord Arthur started, and a faint blush came into his cheek. He had almost entirely forgotten what he had done, and it seemed to him a curious coincidence that Sybil, for whose sake he had gone through all that terrible anxiety, should have been the first to remind him of it.

"Of course you can have it, Sybil. I gave it to poor Lady Clem myself."

"Oh! thank you, Arthur; and may I have the *bonbon* too? I had no notion that Lady Clementina liked sweets. I thought she was far too intellectual."

Lord Arthur grew deadly pale, and a horrible idea crossed his mind.

"*Bonbon*, Sybil? What do you mean?" he said, in a low, hoarse voice.

"There is one in it, that is all. It looks quite old and dusty, and I have not the slightest intention of eating it. What is the matter, Arthur! How white you look!"

Lord Arthur rushed across the room, and seized the box. Inside it was the amber-coloured capsule, with its poison-bubble. Lady Clementina had died a natural death after all!

The shock of the discovery was almost too much for him. He flung the capsule into the fire, and sank on the sofa with a cry of despair.

# V.

Mr. Merton was a good deal distressed at the second postponement of the marriage, and Lady Julia, who had already ordered her dress for the wedding, did all in her power to make Sybil break off the match. Dearly, however, as Sybil loved her mother, she had given her whole life into Lord Arthur's hands, and nothing that Lady Julia could say could make her waver in her faith. As for Lord Arthur himself, it took him days to get over his terrible disappointment, and for a time his nerves were completely unstrung. His excellent common sense, however, soon asserted itself, and his sound, practical mind did not leave him long in doubt about what to do. Poison having proved a complete failure, dynamite, or some other form of explosive, was obviously the proper thing to try.

He accordingly looked again over the list of his friends and relatives, and, after careful consideration, determined to blow up his uncle, the Dean of Chichester. The Dean, who was a man of great culture and learning, was extremely fond of clocks, and had a wonderful collection of timepieces, ranging from the fifteenth century to the present day, and it seemed to Lord Arthur that this hobby of the good Dean's offered him an excellent opportunity for carrying out his scheme. Where to procure an explosive machine was, of course, quite another matter. The London Directory gave him no information on the point, and he felt that there was very little use in going to Scotland Yard about it, as they never seemed to know anything about the movements of the dynamite faction till after an explosion had taken place, and not much even then.

Suddenly he thought of his friend Rouvaloff, a young Russian of very revolutionary tendencies, whom he had met at Lady Windermere's in the winter. Count Rouvaloff was supposed to be writing a life of Peter the Great, and to have come over to England for the purpose of studying the documents relating to that Tsar's resi-

dence in this country as a ship carpenter; but
it was generally suspected that he was a Nihilist
agent, and there was no doubt that the Russian
Embassy did not look with any favour upon his
presence in London.  Lord Arthur felt that he
was just the man for his purpose, and drove
down one morning to his lodgings in Blooms-
bury, to ask his advice and assistance.

"So you are taking up politics seriously?"
said Count Rouvaloff, when Lord Arthur had
told him the object of his mission; but Lord
Arthur, who hated swagger of any kind, felt
bound to admit to him that he had not the
slightest interest in social questions, and simply
wanted the explosive machine for a purely family matter, in which no one was concerned but
himself.

Count Rouvaloff looked at him for some moments in amazement, and then seeing that he
was quite serious, wrote an address on a piece of
paper, initialled it, and handed it to him across
the table.

"Scotland Yard would give a good deal to
know this address, my dear fellow."

"They shan't have it," cried Lord Arthur,
laughing; and after shaking the young Russian

warmly by the hand, he ran downstairs, examined the paper, and told the coachman to drive to Soho Square.

There he dismissed him, and strolled down Greek Street, till he came to a place called Bayle's Court. He passed under the archway, and found himself in a curious *cul-de-sac*, that was apparently occupied by a French Laundry, as a perfect network of clothes-lines was stretched across from house to house, and there was a flutter of white linen in the morning air. He walked right to the end, and knocked at a little green house. After some delay, during which every window in the court became a blurred mass of peering faces, the door was opened by a rather rough-looking foreigner, who asked him in very bad English what his business was. Lord Arthur handed him the paper Count Rouvaloff had given him. When the man saw it he bowed, and invited Lord Arthur into a very shabby front parlour on the ground-floor, and in a few moments Herr Winckelkopf, as he was called in England, bustled into the room, with a very wine-stained napkin round his neck, and a fork in his left hand.

"Count Rouvaloff has given me an introduction to you," said Lord Arthur, bowing, "and I am anxious to have a short interview with you on a matter of business. My name is Smith, Mr. Robert Smith, and I want you to supply me with an explosive clock."

"Charmed to meet you, Lord Arthur," said the genial little German laughing. "Don't look so alarmed, it is my duty to know everybody, and I remember seeing you one evening at Lady Windermere's. I hope her ladyship is quite well. Do you mind sitting with me while I finish my breakfast? There is an excellent *pâté*, and my friends are kind enough to say that my Rhine wine is better than any they get at the German Embassy," and before Lord Arthur had got over his surprise at being recognised, he found himself seated in the back-room, sipping the most delicious Marcobrünner out of a pale yellow hock-glass marked with the Imperial monogram, and chatting in the friendliest manner possible to the famous conspirator.

"Explosive clocks," said Herr Winckelkopf, "are not very good things for foreign exportation, as, even if they succeed in passing the Custom House, the train service is so irregular, that they usually go off before they have reached their proper destination. If, however, you want one for home use, I can supply you with an excellent article, and guarantee that you will be satisfied with the result. May I ask for whom it is intended? If it is for the police, or for any one connected with Scotland Yard, I am afraid I cannot do anything for you. The English detectives are really our best friends, and I have always found that by relying on their stupidity, we can do exactly what we like. I could not spare one of them.''

"I assure you," said Lord Arthur, "that it has nothing to do with the police at all. In fact, the clock is intended for the Dean of Chichester."

"Dear me! I had no idea that you felt so strongly about religion, Lord Arthur. Few young men do nowadays."

"I am afraid you overrate me, Herr Winckelkopf," said Lord Arthur, blushing. "The fact is, I really know nothing about theology."

"It is a purely private matter then?"

"Purely private."

Herr Winckelkopf shrugged his shoulders, and left the room, returning in a few minutes with a round cake of dynamite about the size of

a penny, and a pretty little French clock, sur-
mounted by an ormolu figure of Liberty tramp-
ling on the hydra of Despotism.

Lord Arthur's face brightened up when he
saw it. "That is just what I want," he cried,
"and now tell me how it goes off."

"Ah! there is my secret," answered Herr
Winckelkopf, contemplating his invention with
a justifiable look of pride; "let me know when
you wish it to explode, and I will set the machine to the moment."

"Well, to-day is Tuesday, and if you could
send it off at once——"

"That is impossible; I have a great deal of
important work on hand for some friends of
mine in Moscow. Still, I might send it off to-
morrow."

"Oh, it will be quite time enough!" said
Lord Arthur politely, "If it is delivered to-
morrow night or Thursday morning. For the
moment of the explosion, say Friday at noon
exactly. The Dean is always at home at that
hour."

"Friday, at noon," repeated Herr Winckelkopf, and he made a note to that effect in a large

ledger that was lying on a bureau near the fire-place.

"And now," said Lord Arthur, rising from his seat, "pray let me know how much I am in your debt."

"It is such a small matter, Lord Arthur, that I do not care to make any charge. The dynamite comes to seven and sixpence, the clock will be three pounds ten, and the carriage about five shillings. I am only too pleased to oblige any friend of Count Rouvaloff's."

"But your trouble, Herr Winckelkopf?"

"Oh, that is nothing! It is a pleasure to me. I do not work for money; I live entirely for my art."

Lord Arthur laid down £4:2:6 on the table, thanked the little German for his kindness, and, having succeeded in declining an invitation to meet some Anarchists at a meat-tea on the following Saturday, left the house and went off to the Park.

For the next two days he was in a state of the greatest excitement, and on Friday at twelve o'clock he drove down to the Buckingham to wait for news. All the afternoon the stolid hall-porter kept posting up telegrams from va-

rious parts of the country giving the results of
horse-races, the verdicts in divorce suits, the
state of the weather, and the like, while the tape
ticked out wearisome details about an all-night
sitting in the House of Commons, and a
small Panic on the Stock Exchange. At four
o'clock the evening papers came in, and Lord
Arthur disappeared into the library with the
*Pall Mall*, the *St. James's*, the *Globe*, and the
*Echo*, to the immense indignation of Colonel
Goodchild, who wanted to read the reports of a
speech he had delivered that morning at the
Mansion House, on the subject of South African
Missions, and the advisability of having black
Bishops in every province, and for some reason
or other had a strong prejudice against the
*Evening News*. None of the papers, however,
contained even the slightest allusion to Chichester, and Lord Arthur felt that the attempt must
have failed. It was a terrible blow to him, and
for a time he was quite unnerved. Herr Winckelkopf, whom he went to see the next day, was
full of elaborate apologies, and offered to supply him with another clock free of charge, or
with a case of nitro-glycerine bombs at cost
price. But he had lost all faith in explosives,

and Herr Winckelkopf himself acknowledged that everything is so adulterated nowadays, that even dynamite can hardly be got in a pure condition. The little German, however, while admitting that something must have gone wrong with the machinery, was not without hope that the clock might still go off, and instanced the case of a barometer that he had once sent to the military Governor at Odessa, which, though timed to explode in ten days, had not done so for something like three months. It was quite true that when it did go off, it merely succeeded in blowing a housemaid to atoms, the Governor having gone out of town six weeks before, but at least it showed that dynamite, as a destructive force, was, when under the control of machinery, a powerful, though a somewhat unpunctual agent. Lord Arthur was a little consoled by this reflection, but even here he was destined to disappointment, for two days afterwards, as he was going upstairs, the Duchess called him into her boudoir, and showed him a letter she had just received from the Deanery.

"Jane writes charming letters," said the Duchess; "you must really read her last. It is quite as good as the novels Mudie sends us."

Lord Arthur seized the letter from her hand.
It ran as follows:—

> "THE DEANERY, CHICHESTER,
> "*27th May,*

"My Dearest Aunt,

"Thank you so much for the flannel for the
Dorcas Society, and also for the gingham. I
quite agree with you that it is nonsense their
wanting to wear pretty things, but everybody is
so Radical and irreligious nowadays, that it is
difficult to make them see that they should not
try and dress like the upper classes. I am sure
I don't know what we are coming to. As papa
has often said in his sermons, we live in an age
of unbelief.

"We have had great fun over a clock that an
unknown admirer sent papa last Thursday. It
arrived in a wooden box from London, carriage
paid; and papa feels it must have been sent by
some one who had read his remarkable sermon,
'Is License Liberty?' for on the top of the clock
was a figure of a woman, with what papa said
was the cap of Liberty on her head. I didn't
think it very becoming myself, but papa said it
was historical, so I suppose it is all right. Park-

er unpacked it, and papa put it on the mantelpiece in the library, and we were all sitting there
on Friday morning, when just as the clock
struck twelve, we heard a whirring noise, a little puff of smoke came from the pedestal of the
figure, and the goddess of Liberty fell off, and
broke her nose on the fender!   Maria was quite
alarmed, but it looked so ridiculous, that James
and I went off into fits of laughter, and even
papa was amused.   When we examined it, we
found it was a sort of alarum clock, and that
if you set it to a particular hour, and put some
gunpowder and a cap under a little hammer, it
went off whenever you wanted.   Papa said it
must not remain in the library, as it made a
noise, so Reggie carried it away to the school-
room, and does nothing but have small explo-
sions all day long.   Do you think Arthur would
like one for a wedding present?   I suppose they
are quite fashionable in London.   Papa says
they should do a great deal of good, as they show
that Liberty can't last, but must fall down.
Papa says Liberty was invented at the time of
the French Revolution.   How awful it seems!

"I have now to go to the Dorcas, where I will
read your most instructive letter.   How true,

dear aunt, your idea is, that in their rank of life they should wear what is unbecoming. I must say it is absurd, their anxiety about dress, when there are so many more important things in this world, and in the next. I am so glad your flowered poplin turned out so well, and that your lace was not torn. I am wearing my yellow satin, that you so kindly gave me, at the Bishop's on Wednesday, and think it will look all right. Would you have bows or not? Jennings says that every one wears bows now, and that the underskirt should be frilled. Reggie has just had another explosion, and papa has ordered the clock to be sent to the stables. I don't think papa likes it so much as he did at first, though he is very flattered at being sent such a pretty and ingenious toy. It shows that people read his sermons, and profit by them.

"Papa sends his love, in which James, and Reggie, and Maria all unite, and, hoping that Uncle Cecil's gout is better, believe me, dear aunt, ever your affectionate niece,

JANE PERCY.

"*P. S.*—Do tell me about the bows. Jennings insists they are the fashion."

Lord Arthur looked so serious and unhappy over the letter, that the Duchess went into fits of laughter.

"My dear Arthur," she cried, "I shall never show you a young lady's letter again! But what shall I say about the clock? I think it is a capital invention, and I should like to have one myself."

"I don't think much of them," said Lord Arthur, with a sad smile, and, after kissing his mother, he left the room.

When he got upstairs, he flung himself on a sofa, and his eyes filled with tears. He had done his best to commit this murder, but on both occasions he had failed, and through no fault of his own. He had tried to do his duty, but it seemed as if Destiny herself had turned traitor. He was oppressed with the sense of the barrenness of good intentions, of the futility of trying to be fine. Perhaps, it would be better to break off the marriage altogether. Sybil would suffer, it is true, but suffering could not really mar a nature so noble as hers. As for himself, what did it matter? There is always some war in which a man can die, some cause to which a man can give his life, and as life had no pleasure for him, so death had no terror. Let Destiny work out his doom. He would not stir to help her.

At half-past seven he dressed, and went down to the club. Surbiton was there with a party of young men, and he was obliged to dine with them. Their trivial conversation and idle jests did not interest him, and as soon as coffee was brought he left them, inventing some engagement in order to get away. As he was going out of the club, the hall-porter handed him a letter. It was from Herr Winckelkopf, asking him to call down the next evening, and look at an explosive umbrella, that went off as soon as it was opened. It was the very latest invention, and had just arrived from Geneva. He tore the letter up into fragments. He had made up his mind not to try any more experiments. Then he wandered down to the Thames Embankment, and sat for hours by the river. The moon peered through a mane of tawny clouds, as if it were a lion's eye, and innumerable stars spangled the hollow vault, like gold dust powdered on a purple dome. Now and then a large barge swung out into the turbid stream, and floated away with the tide, and the railway signals changed from green to scarlet as the trains ran shrieking across the bridge. After some time, twelve o'clock boomed from the tall tower at Westminster, and at each stroke of the sonorous bell the night seemed to tremble. Then the railway lights went out, one solitary lamp left gleaming like a large ruby on a giant mast, and the roar of the city became fainter.

At two o'clock he got up, and strolled towards Blackfriars. How unreal everything looked! How like a strange dream! The houses on the other side of the river seemed built out of darkness. One would have said that silver and shadow had fashioned the world anew. The huge dome of St. Paul's loomed like a bubble through the dusky air.

As he approached Cleopatra's Needle he saw a man leaning over the parapet, and as he came nearer the man looked up, the gas-light falling full upon his face.

It was Mr. Podgers, the cheiromantist! No one could mistake the fat, flabby face, the gold-rimmed spectacles, the sickly feeble smile, the sensual mouth.

Lord Arthur stopped. A brilliant idea flashed across him, and he stole softly up behind. In a moment he had seized Mr. Podgers by the legs,

and flung him into the Thames.  There was a
coarse oath, a heavy splash, and all was still.
Lord Arthur looked anxiously over, but could
see nothing of the cheiromantist but a tall hat,
pirouetting in an eddy of moonlit water.  After
a time it also sank, and no trace of Mr. Podgers
was visible.  Once he thought that he caught
sight of the bulky misshapen figure striking out
for the staircase by the bridge, and a horrible
feeling of failure came over him, but it turned
out to be merely a reflection, and when the moon
shone out from behind a cloud it passed away.
At last he seemed to have realised the decree of
destiny.  He heaved a deep sigh of relief, and
Sybil's name came to his lips.

"Have you dropped anything, sir?" said a
voice behind him suddenly.

He turned round, and saw a policeman with
a bull's-eye lantern.

"Nothing of importance, sergeant," he answered, smiling, and hailing a passing hansom,
he jumped in, and told the man to drive to
Belgrave Square.

For the next few days he alternated between
hope and fear.  There were moments when he

almost expected Mr. Podgers to walk into the
room and yet at other times he felt that Fate
could not be so unjust to him. Twice he went
to the cheiromantist's address in West Moon
Street, but he could not bring himself to ring
the bell. He longed for certainty, and was
afraid of it.

Finally it came. He was sitting in the smoking-room of the club having tea, and listening
rather wearily to Surbiton's account of the last
comic song at the Gaiety, when the waiter came
in with the evening papers. He took up the *St.
James's,* and was listlessly turning over its
pages, when this strange heading caught his
eye:

### SUICIDE OF A CHEIROMANTIST.

He turned pale with excitement, and began
to read. The paragraph ran as follows:—

Yesterday morning, at seven o'clock, the body of Mr.
Septimus R. Podgers, the eminent cheiromantist, was
washed on shore at Greenwich, just in front of the Ship
Hotel. The unfortunate gentleman had been missing
for some days, and considerable anxiety for his safety
had been felt in cheiromantic circles. It is supposed
that he committed suicide under the influence of a tem-
porary mental derangement, caused by overwork, and a

verdict to that effect was returned this afternoon by the coroner's jury. Mr. Podgers had just completed an elaborate treatise on the subject of the Human Hand, that will shortly be published, when it will no doubt attract much attention. The deceased was sixty-five years of age, and does not seem to have any relations.

Lord Arthur rushed out of the club with the paper still in his hand, to the immense amazement of the hall-porter, who tried in vain to stop him, and drove at once to Park Lane. Sybil saw him from the window, and something told her that he was the bearer of good news. She ran down to meet him, and, when she saw his face, she knew that all was well.

"My dear Sybil," cried Lord Arthur, "let us be married to-morrow!"

"You foolish boy! Why the cake is not even ordered!" said Sybil, laughing through her tears.

## VI.

When the wedding took place, some three
weeks later, St. Peter's was crowded with a perfect mob of smart people. The service was read
in a most impressive manner by the Dean of
Chichester, and everybody agreed that they had
never seen a handsomer couple than the bride
and bridegroom. They were more than handsome, however—they were happy. Never for a
single moment did Lord Arthur regret all that
he had suffered for Sybil's sake, while she, on
her side, gave him the best things a woman can
give to any man—worship, tenderness, and love.
For them romance was not killed by reality.
They always felt young.

Some years afterwards, when two beautiful
children had been born to them, Lady Win-

dermere came down on a visit to Alton Priory, a lovely old place, that had been the Duke's wedding present to his son; and one afternoon as she was sitting with Lady Arthur under a lime-tree in the garden, watching the little boy and girl as they played up and down the rose-walk, like fitful sunbeams, she suddenly took her hostess's hand in hers, and said, "Are you happy, Sybil?"

"Dear Lady Windermere, of course I am happy. Aren't you?"

"I have no time to be happy, Sybil. I always like the last person who is introduced to me; but, as a rule, as soon as I know people I get tired of them."

"Don't your lions satisfy you, Lady Windermere?"

"Oh dear, no! lions are only good for one season. As soon as their manes are cut, they are the dullest creatures going. Besides, they behave very badly, if you are really nice to them. Do you remember that horrid Mr. Podgers? He was a dreadful impostor. Of course, I didn't mind that at all, and even when he wanted to borrow money I forgave him, but I could not

stand his making love to me. He has really
made me hate cheiromancy. I go in for telepathy
now. It is much more amusing."

"You mustn't say anything against cheiromancy here, Lady Windermere; it is the only
subject that Arthur does not like people to chaff
about. I assure you he is quite serious over it."

"You don't mean to say that he believes in
it, Sybil?"

"Ask him, Lady Windermere, here he is;"
and Lord Arthur came up the garden with a
large bunch of yellow roses in his hand, and
his two children dancing round him.

"Lord Arthur?"

"Yes, Lady Windermere."

"You don't mean to say that you believe in
cheiromancy?"

"Of course I do," said the young man,
smiling.

"But why?"

"Because I owe to it all the happiness of my
life," he murmured, throwing himself into a
wicker chair.

"My dear Lord Arthur, what do you owe to
it?"

"Sybil," he answered, handing his wife the roses, and looking into her violet eyes.

"What nonsense!" cried Lady Windermere. "I never heard such nonsense in all my life."

# The Sphinx Without a Secret.

## An Etching.

# THE SPHINX WITHOUT A SECRET.

One afternoon I was sitting outside the Cafe
de la Paix, watching the splendour and shabbi-
ness of Parisian life, and wondering over my
vermouth at the strange panorama of pride and
poverty that was passing before me, when I heard
some one call my name. I turned round, and
saw Lord Murchison. We had not met since we
had been at college together, nearly ten years
before, so I was delighted to come across him
again, and we shook hands warmly. At Oxford
we had been great friends. I had liked him
immensely, he was so handsome, so high-spirited,
and so honourable. We used to say of him that
he would be the best of fellows, if he did not
always speak the truth, but I think we really
admired him all the more for his frankness. I
found him a good deal changed. He looked
anxious and puzzled, and seemed to be in doubt
about something. I felt it could not be modern

scepticism, for Murchison was the stoutest of
Tories, and believed in the Pentateuch as firmly
as he believed in the House of Peers; so I concluded that it was a woman, and asked him if
he was married yet..

"I don't understand women well enough," he
answered.

"My dear Gerald," I said, "women are meant
to be loved, not to be understood."

"I cannot love where I cannot trust," he
replied.

"I believe you have a mystery in your life,
Gerald," I exclaimed; "tell me about it."

"Let us go for a drive," he answered, "it is
too crowded here. No, not a yellow carriage,
any other colour—there, that dark-green one
will do," and in a few moments we were trot-
ting down the boulevard in the direction of the
Madeleine.

"Where shall we go to?" I said.

"Oh, anywhere you like!" he answered—"to
the restaurant in the Bois; we will dine there,
and you shall tell me all about yourself."

"I want to hear about you first," I said.
"Tell me your mystery."

He took from his pocket a little silver-clasped

morocco case, and handed it to me.  I opened it.
Inside there was the photograph of a woman.
She was tall and slight, and strangely pictur-
esque with her large blue eyes and loosened hair.
She looked like a *clairvoyante,* and was wrapped
in rich furs.

"What do you think of that face?" he said;
"is it truthful?"

I examined it carefully..  It seemed to me the
face of some one who had a secret, but whether
that secret was good or evil I could not say.
Its beauty was a beauty moulded out of many
mysteries—the beauty, in fact, which is psychological, not plastic—and the faint smile that
just played across the lips was far too subtle to
be really sweet.

"Well?" he cried impatiently, "what do you
say?"

"She is the Gioconda in sables," I answered.
"Let me know all about her."

"Not now," he said; "after dinner;" and
began to talk of other things.

When the waiter brought us our coffee and
cigarettes I reminded Gerald of his promise.  He
rose from his seat, walked two or three times up

and down the room, and, sinking into an arm-chair, told me the following story:—

"One evening," he said, "I was walking down Bond Street about five o'clock. There was a terrific crush of carriages, and the traffic was almost stopped. Close to the pavement was standing a little yellow brougham, which, for some reason or other, attracted my attention. As I passed by there looked out from it the face I showed you this afternoon. It fascinated me immediately. All that night I kept thinking of it, and all the next day. I wandered up and down that wretched Row, peering into every carriage, and waiting for the yellow brougham; but I could not find *ma belle inconnue*, and at last I began to think she was merely a dream. About a week afterwards I was dining with Madame de Rastail. Dinner was for eight o'clock; but at half-past eight we were still waiting in the drawing-room. Finally the serv-ant threw open the door, and announced Lady Alroy. It was the woman I had been looking for. She came in very slowly, looking like a moonbeam in grey lace, and, to my intense delight, I was asked to take her in to dinner. After we had sat down I remarked quite innocently, "I think I caught sight of you in Bond Street some time ago, Lady Alroy." She grew very pale, and said to me in a low voice, "Pray do not talk so loud; you may be overheard." I felt miserable at having made such a bad beginning, and plunged recklessly into the subject of the French plays. She spoke very little, always in the same low musical voice, and seemed as if she was afraid of some one listening. I fell passionately, stupidly in love, and the indefinable atmosphere of mystery that surrounded her excited my most ardent curiosity. When she was going away, which she did very soon after dinner, I asked her if I might call and see her. She hesitated for a moment, glanced round to see if any one was near us, and then said, "Yes; to-morrow at a quarter to five." I begged Madame de Rastail to tell me about her; but all that I could learn was that she was a widow with a beautiful house in Park Lane, and as some scientific bore began a dissertation on widows, as exemplifying the survival of the matrimonially fittest, I left and went home.

"The next day I arrived at Park Lane punctual to the moment, but was told by the butler that Lady Alroy had just gone out. I went down to the club quite unhappy and very much puzzled, and after long consideration wrote her a letter, asking if I might be allowed to try my chance some other afternoon. I had no answer for several days, but at last I got a little note saying she would be at home on Sunday at four, and with this extraordinary postscript: "Please do not write to me here again; I will explain when I see you." On Sunday she received me, and was perfectly charming; but when I was going away she begged of me, if I ever had occasion to write to her again, to address my letter to 'Mrs. Knox, care of Whittaker's Library, Green Street.' 'There are reasons,' she said, 'why I cannot receive letters in my own house.'

"All through the season I saw a great deal of her, and the atmosphere of mystery never left her. Sometimes I thought that she was in the power of some man, but she looked so unapproachable that I could not believe it. It was really very difficult for me to come to any conclusion, for she was like one of those strange crystals that one sees in museums, which are at one moment clear, and at another clouded. At last I determined to ask her to be my wife: I was sick and tired of the incessant secrecy that she imposed on all my visits, and on the few letters I sent her. I wrote to her at the library to ask her if she could see me the following Monday at six. She answered yes, and I was in the seventh heaven of delight. I was infatuated with her: in spite of the mystery, I thought then—in consequence of it, I see now. No; it was the woman herself I loved. The mystery troubled me, maddened me. Why did chance put me in its track?"

"You discovered it, then?" I cried.

"I fear so," he answered. "You can judge for yourself."

"When Monday came round I went to lunch with my uncle, and about four o'clock found myself in the Marylebone Road. My uncle, you know, lives in Regent's Park. I wanted to get to Piccadilly, and took a short cut through a lot of shabby little streets. Suddenly I saw in front of me Lady Alroy, deeply veiled and walking very fast. On coming to the last house in the street, she went up the steps, took out a latch-key, and let herself in. 'Here is the mystery,'

I said to myself; and I hurried on and examined the house. It seemed a sort of place for letting lodgings. On the doorstep lay her handkerchief, which she had dropped. I picked it up and put it in my pocket. Then I began to consider what I should do. I came to the conclusion that I had no right to spy on her, and I drove down to the club. At six I called to see her. She was lying on a sofa, in a tea-gown of silver tissue looped up by some strange moonstones that she always wore. She was looking quite lovely. 'I am so glad to see you,' she said; 'I have not been out all day.' I stared at her in amazement, and pulling the handkerchief out of my pocket, handed it to her. 'You dropped this in Cumnor Street this afternoon, Lady Alroy,' I said very calmly. She looked at me in terror, but made no attempt to take the handkerchief. 'What were you doing there?' I asked. 'What right have you to question me?' she answered. 'The right of a man who loves you,' I replied; 'I came here to ask you to be my wife.' She hid her face in her hands, and burst into floods of tears. 'You must tell me,' I continued. She stood up, and, looking me

'Can't you tell the truth,' I exclaimed.'
Page 83

I said to myself; and I returned on and examine the house. It seemed a sort of place for her lodgings. On the doorstep lay her hand-kerchief, which she had dropped. I picked it and put it in my pocket. Then I began to ask myself what I should do. I came to the conclusion that I had no right to spy on her, and I drove down to the club. At six I called to see her. She was lying on a sofa, in a tea-gown of silver tissue looped up by some strange moonstones that she always wore. She was looking lovely. 'I am so glad to see you,' she said, 'I have not been out all day.' I stared at her in amazement, and pulling the handkerchief out, handed it to her. 'You dropped this in Cumnor Street this afternoon, Gladys,' I said very calmly. She looked at me in horror, but made no attempt to take the handkerchief. 'What were you doing there?' I asked. 'What right have you to question me?' she replied. 'The right of a man who loves you,' I answered; 'I came here to ask you to be my wife.' She hid her face in her hands, and burst into floods of tears. 'You must tell me,' I continued. She stood up, and looking

straight in the face, said, 'Lord Murchison, there is nothing to tell you.'—'You went to meet some one,' I cried; 'this is your mystery.' She grew dreadfully white, and said, 'I went to meet no one.'—'Can't you tell the truth?' I exclaimed. 'I have told it,' she replied. I was mad, frantic; I don't know what I said, but I said terrible things to her. Finally I rushed out of the house. She wrote me a letter the next day; I sent it back unopened, and started for Norway with Alan Colville. After a month I came back, and the first thing I saw in the *Morning Post* was the death of Lady Alroy. She had caught a chill at the Opera, and had died in five days of congestion of the lungs. I shut myself up and saw no one. I had loved her so much, I had loved her so madly. Good God! how I had loved that woman!"

"You went to the street, to the house in it?" I said.

"Yes," he answered.

"One day I went to Cumnor Street. I could not help it; I was tortured with doubt. I knocked at the door, and a respectable-looking woman opened it to me. I asked her if she had any rooms to let. 'Well, sir,' she replied, 'the drawing-rooms are supposed to be let; but I have not seen the lady for three months, and as rent is owing on them, you can have them.'—'Is this the lady?' I said, showing the photograph. 'That's her, sure enough,' she exclaimed; 'and when is she coming back, sir?'—'The lady is dead,' I replied. 'Oh, sir, I hope not!' said the woman; 'she was my best lodger. She paid me three guineas a week merely to sit in my drawing-rooms now and then.'—'She met some one here?' I said; but the woman assured me that it was not so, that she always came alone, and saw no one. 'What on earth did she do here?' I cried. 'She simply sat in the drawing-room, sir, reading books, and sometimes had tea,' the woman answered. I did not know what to say, so I gave her a sovereign and went away. Now, what do you think it all means? You don't believe the woman was telling the truth?''

"I do."

"Then why did Lady Alroy go there?"

"My dear Gerald," I answered, "Lady Alroy was simply a woman with a mania for mystery. She took these rooms for the pleasure of going there with her veil down, and imagining she was a heroine. She had a passion for secrecy, but she herself was merely a Sphinx without a secret.''

''Do you really think so?''

''I am sure of it,'' I replied.

He took out the morocco case, opened it, and looked at the photograph. ''I wonder?'' he said at last.

# The Canterville Ghost.

## A Hylo-Idealistic Romance.

# THE CANTERVILLE GHOST.

## I.

When Mr. Hiram B. Otis, the American Minister, bought Canterville Chase, every one told him he was doing a very foolish thing, as there was no doubt at all that the place was haunted. Indeed, Lord Canterville himself, who was a man of the most punctllious honour, had felt it his duty to mention the fact to Mr. Otis when they came to discuss terms.

"We have not cared to live in the place ourselves," said Lord Canterville, "since my grand-aunt, the Dowager Duchess of Bolton, was frightened into a fit, from which she never really recovered, by two skeleton hands being placed on her shoulders as she was dressing for dinner, and I feel bound to tell you, Mr. Otis, that the ghost has been seen by several living members of my family, as well as by the rector of the parish, Rev. Augustus Dampier, who is a Fellow of King's College, Cambridge. After the unfortunate accident to the Duchess, none of our younger servants would stay with us, and Lady Canterville often got very little sleep at night, in consequence of the mysterious noises that came from the corridor and the library.''

''My Lord,'' answered the Minister, ''I will take the furniture and the ghost at a valuation. I come from a modern country, where we have everything that money can buy; and with all our spry young fellows painting the Old World red, and carrying off your best actors and prima-donnas, I reckon that if there were such a thing as a ghost in Europe, we'd have it at home in a very short time in one of our public museums, or on the road as a show.''

''I fear that the ghost exists,'' said Lord Canterville, smiling, ''though it may have resisted the overtures of your enterprising impresarios. It has been well known for three centuries, since 1584 in fact, and always makes its appearance before the death of any member of our family.''

''Well, so does the family doctor for that matter, Lord Canterville. But there is no such thing, sir, as a ghost, and I guess the laws of

Nature are not going to be suspended for the British aristocracy.''

"You are certainly very natural in America,'' answered Lord Canterville, who did not quite understand Mr. Otis's last observation, ''and if you don't mind a ghost in the house, it is all right. Only you must remember I warned you.''

A few weeks after this, the purchase was concluded, and at the close of the season the Minister and his family went down to Canterville Chase. Mrs. Otis, who, as Miss Lucretia R. Tappan, of West 53d Street, had been a celebrated New York belle, was now a very handsome, middle-aged woman, with fine eyes, and a superb profile. Many American ladies on leaving their native land adopt an appearance of chronic ill-health, under the impression that it is a form of European refinement, but Mrs. Otis had never fallen into this error. She had a magnificent constitution, and a really wonderful amount of animal spirits. Indeed, in many respects, she was quite English, and was an excellent example of the fact that we have really everything in common with America nowadays, except, of course, language. Her eldest son, christened Washington by his parents in a moment of patriotism, which he never ceased to regret, was a fair-haired, rather good-looking young man, who had qualified himself for American diplomacy by leading the German at the Newport Casino for three successive seasons, and even in London was well known as an excellent dancer. Gardenias and the peerage were his only weaknesses. Otherwise he was extremely sensible. Miss Virginia E. Otis was a little girl of fifteen, lithe and lovely as a fawn, and with a fine freedom in her large blue eyes. She was a wonderful amazon, and had once raced old Lord Bilton on her pony twice round the park, winning by a length and a half, just in front of the Achilles statue, to the huge delight of the young Duke of Cheshire, who proposed for her on the spot, and was sent back to Eton that very night by his guardians, in floods of tears. After Virginia came the twins, who were usually called the "Stars and Stripes," as they were always getting swished. They were delightful boys, and with the exception of the worthy Minister the only true republicans of the family.

As Canterville Chase is seven miles from

Ascot, the nearest railway station, Mr. Otis had telegraphed for a waggonette to meet them, and they started on the drive in high spirits. It was a lovely July evening, and the air was delicate with the scent of the pinewoods. Now and then they heard a wood pigeon brooding over its own sweet voice, or saw, deep in the rustling fern, the burnished breast of the pheasant. Little squirrels peered at them from the beech-trees as they went by, and the rabbits scudded away through the brushwood and over the mossy knolls, with their white tails in the air. As they entered the avenue of Canterville Chase, however, the sky became suddenly overcast with clouds, a curious stillness seemed to hold the atmosphere, a great flight of rooks passed silently over their heads, and, before they reached the house, some big drops of rain had fallen.

Standing on the steps to receive them was an old woman, neatly dressed in black silk, with a white cap and apron. This was Mrs. Umney, the housekeeper, whom Mrs. Otis, at Lady Canterville's earnest request, had consented to keep on in her former position. She made them each a low courtesy as they alighted, and said in a quaint, old-fashioned manner, "I bid you welcome to Canterville Chase." Following her, they passed through the fine Tudor hall into the library, a long, low room, panelled in black oak, at the end of which was a large stained-glass window. Here they found tea laid out for them, and, after taking off their wraps, they sat down and began to look round, while Mrs. Umney waited on them.

Suddenly Mrs. Otis caught sight of a dull red stain on the floor just by the fireplace and, quite unconscious of what it really signified, said to Mrs. Umney, "I am afraid something has been spilt there."

"Yes, madam," replied the old housekeeper in a low voice, "blood has been spilt on that spot."

"How horrid," cried Mrs. Otis; "I don't at all care for blood-stains in a sitting-room. It must be removed at once."

The old woman smiled, and answered in the same low, mysterious voice, "It is the blood of Lady Eleanore de Canterville, who was murdered on that very spot by her own husband, Sir Simon de Canterville, in 1575. Sir Simon survived her nine years, and disappeared suddenly under very mysterious circumstances. His body has never been discovered, but his guilty spirit still haunts the Chase. The blood-stain has been much admired by tourists and others, and cannot be removed."

"That is all nonsense," cried Washington Otis; "Pinkerton's Champion Stain Remover and Paragon Detergent will clean it up in no time," and before the terrified housekeeper could interfere he had fallen upon his knees, and was rapidly scouring the floor with a small stick of what looked like a black cosmetic. In a few moments no trace of the blood-stain could be seen.

"I knew Pinkerton would do it," he exclaimed triumphantly, as he looked round at his admiring family; but no sooner had he said these words than a terrible flash of lightning lit up the sombre room, a fearful peal of thunder made them all start to their feet, and Mrs. Umney fainted.

"What a monstrous climate!" said the American Minister calmly, as he lit a long cheroot. "I guess the old country is so over-populated that they have not enough decent weather for everybody. I have always been of opinion that emigration is the only thing for England."

"My dear Hiram," cried Mrs. Otis, "what can we do with a woman who faints?"

"Charge it to her like breakages," answered the Minister; "she won't faint after that;" and in a few moments Mrs. Umney certainly came to. There was no doubt, however, that she was extremely upset, and she sternly warned Mr. Otis to beware of some trouble coming to the house.

"I have seen things with my own eyes, sir," she said, "that would make any Christian's hair stand on end, and many and many a night I have not closed my eyes in sleep for the awful things that are done here." Mr. Otis, however, and his wife warmly assured the honest soul that they were not afraid of ghosts, and, after invoking the blessings of Providence on her new master and mistress, and making arrangements for an increase of salary, the old housekeeper tottered off to her own room.

## II.

The storm raged fiercely all that night, but
nothing of particular note occurred. The next
morning, however, when they came down to
breakfast, they found the terrible stain of blood
once again on the floor. "I don't think it can
be the fault of the Paragon Detergent," said
Washington, "for I have tried it with everything. It must be the ghost." He accordingly
rubbed out the stain a second time, but the
second morning it appeared again. The third
morning also it was there, though the library
had been locked up at night by Mr. Otis himself,
and the key carried upstairs. The whole family
were now quite interested; Mr. Otis began to
suspect that he had been too dogmatic in his
denial of the existence of ghosts, Mrs. Otis
expressed her intention of joining the Psychical

97

Society, and Washington prepared a long letter to Messrs. Myers and Podmore on the subject of the Permanence of Sanguineous Stains when connected with Crime. That night all doubts about the objective existence of phantasmata were removed for ever.

The day had been warm and sunny; and, in the cool of the evening, the whole family went out to drive. They did not return home till nine o'clock, when they had a light supper. The conversation in no way turned upon ghosts, so there were not even those primary conditions of receptive expectation which so often precede the presentation of psychical phenomena. The subjects discussed, as I have since learned from Mr. Otis, were merely such as form the ordinary conversation of cultured Americans of the better class, such as the immense superiority of Miss Fanny Davenport over Sara Bernhardt as an actress; the difficulty of obtaining green corn, buckwheat cakes, and hominy, even in the best English houses; the importance of Boston in the development of the world-soul; the advantages of the baggage check system in railway travelling; and the sweetness of the New York accent as compared to the London drawl. No mention at all was made of the supernatural, nor was Sir Simon de Canterville alluded to in any way. At eleven o'clock the family retired, and by half-past all the lights were out. Some time after, Mr. Otis was awakened by a curious noise in the corridor, outside his room. It sounded like the clank of metal, and seemed to be coming nearer every moment. He got up at once, struck a match, and looked at the time. It was exactly one o'clock. He was quite calm, and felt his pulse, which was not at all feverish. The strange noise still continued, and with it he heard distinctly the sound of footsteps. He put on his slippers, took a small oblong phial out of his dressing-case, and opened the door. Right in front of him he saw, in the wan moonlight, an old man of terrible aspect. His eyes were as red as burning coals; long grey hair fell over his shoulders in matted coils; his garments, which were of antique cut, were soiled and ragged, and from his wrists and ankles hung heavy manacles and rusty gyves.

"My dear sir," said Mr. Otis, "I really must insist on your oiling those chains, and have brought you for that purpose a small bottle of the Tammany Rising Sun Lubricator. It is said to be completely efficacious upon one application, and there are several testimonials to that effect on the wrapper from some of our most eminent native divines. I shall leave it here for you by my bedroom candles, and will be happy to supply you with more should you require it." With these words the United States Minister laid the bottle down on a marble table, and, closing the door, retired to rest.

For a moment the Canterville ghost stood quite motionless in natural indignation; then, dashing the bottle violently upon the polished floor, he fled down the corridor, uttering hollow groans, and emitting a ghastly green light. Just, however, as he reached the top of the great oak staircase, a door was flung open, two little white-robed figures appeared, and a large pillow whizzed past his head! There was evidently no time to be lost, so, hastily adopting the Fourth Dimension of Space as a means of escape, he vanished through the wainscoting, and the house became quite quiet.

On reaching a small secret chamber in the left wing, he leaned up against a moonbeam to recover his breath, and began to try and realise his position. Never, in a brilliant and uninter-

rupted career of three hundred years, had he
been so grossly insulted. He thought of the
Dowager Duchess, whom he had frightened into
a fit as she stood before the glass in her lace and
diamonds; of the four housemaids, who had
gone off into hysterics when he merely grinned
at them through the curtains of one of the spare
bedrooms; of the rector of the parish, whose
candle he had blown out as he was coming late
one night from the library, and who had been
under the care of Sir William Gull ever since, a
perfect martyr to nervous disorders; and of old
Madame de Tremouillac, who, having wakened
up one morning early and seen a skeleton seated
in an armchair by the fire reading her diary,
had been confined to her bed for six weeks with
an attack of brain fever, and, on her recovery,
had become reconciled to the Church, and broken
off her connection with that notorious sceptic
Monsieur de Voltaire. He remembered the terrible night when the wicked Lord Canterville
was found choking in his dressing-room, with
the knave of diamonds half-way down his throat,
and confessed, just before he died, that he had
cheated Charles James Fox out of £50,000 at

Crockford's by means of that very card, and swore that the ghost had made him swallow it. All his great achievements came back to him again, from the butler who had shot himself in the pantry because he had seen a green hand tapping at the window pane, to the beautiful Lady Stutfield, who was always obliged to wear a black velvet band round her throat to hide the mark of five fingers burnt upon her white skin, and who drowned herself at last in the carp-pond at the end of the King's Walk. With the enthusiastic egotism of the true artist he went over his most celebrated performances, and smiled bitterly to himself as he recalled to mind his last appearance as "Red Reuben, or the Strangled Babe," his *début* as "Gaunt Gibeon, the Blood-sucker of Bexley Moor," and the *furore* he had excited one lovely June evening by merely playing ninepins with his own bones upon the lawn-tennis ground. And after all this, some wretched modern Americans were to come and offer him the Rising Sun Lubricator, and throw pillows at his head! It was quite unbearable. Besides, no ghost in history had ever been treated in this manner. Accordingly, he determined to have vengeance, and remained till daylight in an attitude of deep thought.

## III.

The next morning, when the Otis family met at breakfast, they discussed the ghost at some length. The United States Minister was naturally a little annoyed to find that his present had not been accepted. "I have no wish," he said, "to do the ghost any personal injury, and I must say that, considering the length of time he has been in the house, I don't think it is at all polite to throw pillows at him"—a very just remark, at which I am sorry to say, the twins burst into shouts of laughter. "Upon the other hand," he continued, "if he really declines to use the Rising Sun Lubricator, we shall have to take his chains from him. It would be quite impossible to sleep, with such a noise going on outside the bedrooms."

For the rest of the week, however, they were

undisturbed, the only thing that excited any attention being the continual renewal of the blood-stain on the library floor. This certainly was very strange, as the door was always locked at night by Mr. Otis, and the windows kept closely barred. The chameleon-like colour, also, of the stain excited a good deal of comment. Some mornings it was a dull (almost Indian) red, then it would be vermilion, then a rich purple, and once when they came down for family prayers, according to the simple rites of the Free American Reformed Episcopalian Church, they found it a bright emerald-green. These kaleidoscopic changes naturally amused the party very much, and bets on the subject were freely made every evening. The only person who did not enter into the joke was little Virginia, who, for some unexplained reason, was always a good deal distressed at the sight of the blood-stain, and very nearly cried the morning it was emerald-green.

The second appearance of the ghost was on Sunday night. Shortly after they had gone to bed they were suddenly alarmed by a fearful crash in the hall. Rushing downstairs, they found that a large suit of old armour had become

detached from its stand, and had fallen on the
stone floor, while, seated in a high-backed chair,
was the Canterville ghost, rubbing his knees
with an expression of acute agony on his face.
The twins, having brought their pea-shooters
with them, at once discharged two pellets on
him, with that accuracy of aim which can only
be attained by long and careful practice on a
writing-master, while the United States Minister
covered him with a revolver, and called upon
him, in accordance with Californian etiquette,
to hold up his hands!  The ghost started up
with a wild shriek of rage, and swept through
them like a mist, extinguishing Washington
Otis's candle as he passed, and so leaving them
all in total darkness.  On reaching the top of
the staircase he recovered himself, and determined to give his celebrated peal of demoniac
laughter.  This he had on more than one occasion
found extremely useful.  It was said to have
turned Lord Raker's wig grey in a single night,
and had certainly made three of Lady Canterville's French governesses give warning before
their month was up.  He accordingly laughed
his most horrible laugh, till the old vaulted roof
rang and rang again, but hardly had the fearful

echo died away when a door opened, and Mrs. Otis came out in a light blue dressing-gown. "I am afraid you are far from well," she said, "and have brought you a bottle of Dr. Dobell's tincture. If it is indigestion, you will find it a most excellent remedy." The ghost glared at her in fury, and began at once to make preparations for turning himself into a large black dog, an accomplishment for which he was justly renowned, and to which the family doctor always attributed the permanent idiocy of Lord Canterville's uncle, the Hon. Thomas Horton. The sound of approaching footsteps, however, made him hesitate in his fell purpose, so he contented himself with becoming faintly phosphorescent, and vanished with a deep churchyard groan, just as the twins had come up to him.

On reaching his room he entirely broke down, and became a prey to the most violent agitation. The vulgarity of the twins, and the gross materialism of Mrs. Otis, were naturally extremely annoying, but what really distressed him most was, that he had been unable to wear the suit of mail. He had hoped that even modern Americans would be thrilled by the sight of a Spectre In Armour, if for no more

sensible reason, at least out of respect for their
national poet Longfellow, over whose graceful
and attractive poetry he himself had whiled
away many a weary hour when the Cantervilles
were up in town.  Besides, it was his own suit.
He had worn it with great success at the Kenil-
worth tournament, and had been highly complimented on it by no less a person than the Virgin
Queen herself.  Yet when he had put it on, he
had been completely overpowered by the weight
of the huge breastplate and steel casque, and
had fallen heavily on the stone pavement, bark-
ing both his knees severely, and bruising the
knuckles of his right hand.

For some days after this he was extremely ill,
and hardly stirred out of his room at all, except
to keep the blood-stain in proper repair.  However, by taking great care of himself, he recovered, and resolved to make a third attempt to
frighten the United States Minister and his
family.  He selected Friday, the 17th of August,
for his appearance, and spent most of that day
in looking over his wardrobe, ultimately decid-
ing in favour of a large slouched hat with a red
feather, a winding-sheet frilled at the wrists
and neck, and a rusty dagger.  Towards evening

a violent storm of rain came on, and the wind
was so high that all the windows and doors in
the old house shook and rattled. In fact, it was
just such weather as he loved. His plan of
action was this. He was to make his way quietly
to Washington Otis's room, gibber at him from
the foot of the bed, and stab himself three times
in the throat to the sound of low music. He
bore Washington a special grudge, being quite
aware that it was he who was in the habit of
removing the famous Canterville blood-stain, by
means of Pinkerton's Paragon Detergent. Having reduced the reckless and foolhardy youth
to a condition of abject terror, he was then to
proceed to the room occupied by the United
States Minister and his wife, and there to place
a clammy hand on Mrs. Otis's forehead, while
he hissed into her trembling husband's ear the
awful secrets of the charnel-house. With regard
to little Virginia, he had not quite made up his
mind. She had never insulted him in any way,
and was pretty and gentle. A few hollow groans
from the wardrobe, he thought, would be more
than sufficient, or, if that failed to wake her, he
might grabble at the counterpane with palsy-
twitching fingers. As for the twins, he was

quite determined to teach them a lesson.   The
first thing to be done was, of course, to sit upon
their chests, so as to produce the stifling sensation of nightmare.   Then, as their beds were
quite close to each other, to stand between them
in the form of a green, icy-cold corpse, till they
became paralysed with fear, and finally,
to throw off the winding-sheet, and crawl round
the room, with white, bleached bones and one
rolling eyeball, in the character of "Dumb
Daniel, or the Suicide's Skeleton," a *rôle* in
which he had on more than one occasion produced a great effect, and which he considered
quite equal to his famous part of "Martin the
Maniac, or the Masked Mystery."

At half-past ten he heard the family going to
bed.   For some time he was disturbed by wild
shrieks of laughter from the twins, who with the
light-hearted gaiety of school-boys, were evidently amusing themselves before they retired
to rest, but at a quarter past eleven all was still,
and, as midnight sounded, he sallied forth.   The
owl beat against the window panes, the raven
croaked from the old yew-tree, and the wind
wandered moaning round the house like a lost
soul; but the Otis family slept unconscious of

their doom, and high above the rain and storm
he could hear the steady snoring of the Minister
of the United States. He stepped stealthily
out of the wainscoting, with an evil smile on his
cruel, wrinkled mouth, and the moon hid her
face in a cloud as he stole past the great oriel
window, where his own arms and those of his
murdered wife were blazoned in azure and gold.
On and on he glided, like an evil shadow,
the very darkness seeming to loathe him as he
passed. Once he thought he heard something
call, and stopped; but it was only the baying
of a dog from the Red Farm, and he went on,
muttering strange sixteenth-century curses, and
ever and anon brandishing the rusty dagger in
the midnight air. Finally he reached the corner
of the passage that led to luckless Washington's
room. For a moment he paused there, the wind
blowing his long grey locks about his head, and
twisting into grotesque and fantastic folds the
nameless horror of the dead man's shroud. Then
the clock struck the quarter, and he felt the time
was come. He chuckled to himself, and turned
the corner; but no sooner had he done so, than,
with a piteous wail of terror, he fell back, and

hid his blanched face in his long, bony hands.
Right in front of him was standing a horrible
spectre, motionless as a carven image, and monstrous as a madman's dream! Its head was bald
and burnished; its face round, and fat, and
white; and hideous laughter seemed to have
writhed its features into an eternal grin. From
the eyes streamed rays of scarlet light, the mouth
was a wide well of fire, and a hideous garment,
like to his own, swathed with its silent snows
the Titan form. On its breast was a placard
with strange writing in antique characters, some
scroll of shame it seemed, some record of wild
sins, some awful calendar of crime, and, with
its right hand, it bore aloft a falchion of gleaming steel.

Never having seen a ghost before, he naturally
was terribly frightened, and, after a second
hasty glance at the awful phantom, he fled back
to his room, tripping up in his long winding
sheet as he sped down the corridor, and finally
dropping the rusty dagger into the Minister's
jack-boots, where it was found in the morning
by the butler. Once in the privacy of his own
apartment, he flung himself down on a small

pallet-bed, and hid his face under the clothes. After a time, however, the brave old Canterville spirit asserted itself, and he determined to go and speak to the other ghost as soon as it was daylight. Accordingly, just as the dawn was touching the hills with silver, he returned towards the spot where he had first laid eyes on the grisly phantom, feeling that, after all, two ghosts were better than one, and that, by the aid of his new friend, he might safely grapple with the twins. On reaching the spot, however, a terrible sight met his gaze. Something had evidently happened to the spectre, for the light had entirely faded from its hollow eyes, the gleaming falchion had fallen from its hand, and it was leaning up against the wall in a strained and uncomfortable attitude. He rushed forward and seized it in his arms, when, to his horror, the head slipped off and rolled on the floor, the body assumed a recumbent posture, and he found himself clasping a white dimity bedcurtain, with a sweeping-brush, a kitchen cleaver, and a hollow turnip lying at his feet! Unable to understand this curious transformation, he clutched the placard with feverish haste, and

there, in the grey morning light, he read these
fearful words:—

> ### YE OTIS GHOSTE.
> #### Ye onlie True and Originale Spook.
> #### Beware of Ye Imitationes.
> #### All others are Counterfeite.

The whole thing flashed across him.  He had
been tricked, foiled, and outwitted!  The old
Canterville look came into his eyes; he ground
his toothless gums together; and, raising his
withered hands high above his head, swore, according to the picturesque phraseology of the
antique school, that when Chanticleer had
sounded twice his merry horn, deeds of blood
would be wrought, and Murder walk abroad
with silent feet.

Hardly had he finished this awful oath when,
from the red-tiled roof of a distant homestead,
a cock crew.  He laughed a long, low, bitter
laugh, and waited.  Hour after hour he waited,
but the cock, for some strange reason, did not
crow again.  Finally, at half-past seven, the arrival of the housemaids made him give up his

fearful vigil, and he stalked back to his room, thinking of his vain oath and baffled purpose. There he consulted several books of ancient chivalry, of which he was exceedingly fond, and found that, on every occasion on which this oath had been used, Chanticleer had always crowed a second time. "Perdition seize the naughty fowl," he muttered, "I have seen the day when, with my stout spear, I would have run him through the gorge, and made him crow for me an 'twere in death!" He then retired to a comfortable lead coffin, and stayed there till evening.

## IV.

The next day the ghost was very weak and
tired. The terrible excitement of the last four
weeks was beginning to have its effect. His
nerves were completely shattered, and he started
at the slightest noise. For five days he kept his
room, and at last made up his mind to give up
the point of the blood-stain on the library floor.
If the Otis family did not want it, they clearly
did not deserve it. They were evidently people
on a low, material plane of existence, and quite
incapable of appreciating the symbolic value of
sensuous phenomena. The question of phan-
tasmic apparitions, and the development of as-
tral bodies, was of course quite a different matter, and really not under his control. It was
his solemn duty to appear in the corridor once a
week, and to gibber from the large oriel window
117

on the first and third Wednesdays in every month, and he did not see how he could honourably escape from his obligations. It is quite true that his life had been very evil, but, upon the other hand, he was most conscientious in all things connected with the supernatural. For the next three Saturdays, accordingly, he traversed the corridor as usual between midnight and three o'clock, taking every possible precaution against being either heard or seen. He removed his boots, trod as lightly as possible on the old worm-eaten boards, wore a large black velvet cloak, and was careful to use the Rising Sun Lubricator for oiling his chains. I am bound to acknowledge that it was with a good deal of difficulty that he brought himself to adopt this last mode of protection. However, one night, while the family were at dinner, he slipped into Mr. Otis's bedroom and carried off the bottle. He felt a little humiliated at first, but afterwards was sensible enough to see that there was a great deal to be said for the invention, and, to a certain degree, it served his purpose. Still, in spite of everything, he was not left unmolested. Strings were continually being stretched across the corridor, over which he tripped in the dark, and on one occasion, while dressed for the part of "Black Isaac, or the Huntsman of Hogley Woods," he met with a severe fall, through treading on a butter-slide, which the twins had constructed from the entrance of the Tapestry Chamber to the top of the oak staircase.   This last insult so enraged him, that he resolved to make one final effort to assert his dignity and social position, and determined to visit the insolent young Etonians the next night in his celebrated character of "Reckless Rupert, or the Headless Earl."

He had not appeared in this disguise for more than seventy years: in fact, not since he had so frightened pretty Lady Barbara Modish by means of it, that she suddenly broke off her engagement with the present Lord Canterville's grandfather, and ran away to Gretna Green with handsome Jack Castletown, declaring that nothing in the world would induce her to marry into a family that allowed such a horrible phantom to walk up and down the terrace at twilight.   Poor Jack was afterwards shot in a duel by Lord Canterville on Wandsworth Common, and Lady Barbara died of a broken heart at Tunbridge Wells before the year was out, so, in every way, it had been a great success. It was, however, an extremely difficult "make-up," if I may use such a theatrical expression in connection with one of the greatest mysteries of the supernatural, or, to employ a more scientific term, the higher-natural world, and it took him fully three hours to make his preparations. At last everything was ready, and he was very pleased with his appearance. The big leather riding-boots that went with the dress were just a little too large for him, and he could only find one of the two horse-pistols, but, on the whole, he was quite satisfied, and at a quarter past one he glided out of the wainscoting and crept down the corridor. On reaching the room occupied by the twins, which I should mention was called the Blue Bed Chamber, on account of the colour of its hangings, he found the door just ajar. Wishing to make an effective entrance, he flung it wide open, when a heavy jug of water fell right down on him, wetting him to the skin, and just missing his left shoulder by a couple of inches. At the same moment he heard stifled shrieks of laughter proceeding from the four-post bed. The shock to his nervous system was so great that he fled back to his room as hard

as he could go, and the next day he was laid up
with a severe cold. The only thing that at all
consoled him in the whole affair was the fact
that he had not brought his head with him, for,
had he done so, the consequences might have
been very serious.

He now gave up all hope of ever frightening
this rude American family, and contented himself, as a rule, with creeping about the passages
in list slippers, with a thick red muffler round
his throat for fear of draughts, and a small
arquebuse, in case he should be attacked by the
twins. The final blow he received occurred on
the 19th of September. He had gone downstairs to the great entrance-hall, feeling sure
that there, at any rate, he would be quite unmolested, and was amusing himself by making sa-
tirical remarks on the large Saroni photographs
of the United States Minister and his wife,
which had now taken the place of the Canterville family pictures. He was simply but neatly
clad in a long shroud, spotted with churchyard
mould, had tied up his jaw with a strip of yellow linen, and carried a small lantern and a
sexton's spade. In fact, he was dressed for the
character of "Jonas the Graveless, or the

Corpse-Snatcher of Chertsey Barn,'' one of his most remarkable impersonations, and one which the Cantervilles had every reason to remember, as it was the real origin of their quarrel with their neighbour, Lord Rufford. It was about a quarter past two o'clock in the morning, and, as far as he could ascertain, no one was stirring. As he was strolling towards the library, however, to see if there were any traces left of the blood-stain, suddenly there leaped out on him from a dark corner two figures, who waved their arms wildly above their heads, and shrieked out "BOO!" in his ear.

Seized with a panic, which, under the circumstances, was only natural, he rushed for the staircase, but found Washington Otis waiting for him there with the big garden-syringe; and being thus hemmed in by his enemies on every side, and driven almost to bay, he vanished into the great iron stove, which, fortunately for him, was not lit, and had to make his way home through the flues and chimneys, arriving at his own room in a terrible state of dirt, disorder, and despair.

After this he was not seen again on any nocturnal expedition. The twins lay in wait for him on several occasions, and strewed the passages with nutshells every night to the great annoyance of their parents and the servants, but it was of no avail.  It was quite evident that his feelings were so wounded that he would not appear.  Mr. Otis consequently resumed his great work on the history of the Democratic Party, on which he had been engaged for some years; Mrs. Otis organized a wonderful clam-bake, which amazed the whole county; the boys took to lacrosse, euchre, poker, and other American national games; and Virginia rode about the lanes on her pony, accompanied by the young Duke of Cheshire, who had come to spend the last week of his holidays at Canterville Chase.   It was generally assumed that the ghost had gone away, and, in fact, Mr. Otis wrote a letter to that effect to Lord Canterville, who, in reply, expressed his great pleasure at the news, and sent his best congratulations to the Minister's worthy wife.

The Otises, however, were deceived, for the ghost was still in the house, and though now almost an invalid, was by no means ready to let matters rest, particularly as he heard that among the guests was the young Duke of Cheshire, whose grand-uncle, Lord Francis Stilton had

once bet a hundred guineas with Colonel Car-
bury that he would play dice with the Canterville ghost, and was found next morning lying
on the floor of the card-room in such a helpless
paralytic state, that though he lived on to a
great age, he was never able to say anything
again but "Double Sixes." The story was well
known at the time, though, of course, out of
respect to the feelings of the two noble families,
every attempt was made to hush it up ; and a full
account of all the circumstances connected with
it will be found in the third volume of Lord
Tattle's *Recollections of the Prince Regent and
his Friends*. The ghost, then, was naturally
very anxious to show that he had not lost his influence over the Stiltons, with whom, indeed,
he was distantly connected, his own first cousin
having been married *en secondes noces* to the
Sieur de Bulkeley, from whom, as every one
knows, the Dukes of Cheshire are lineally de-
scended. Accordingly, he made arrangements
for appearing to Virginia's little lover in his
celebrated impersonation of "The Vampire
Monk, or the Bloodless Benedictine," a performance so horrible that when old Lady Startup
saw it, which she did on one fatal New Year's

Eve, in the year 1764, she went off into the most piercing shrieks, which culminated in violent apoplexy, and died in three days, after disinheriting the Cantervilles, who were her nearest relations, and leaving all her money to her London apothecary. At the last moment, however, his terror of the twins prevented his leaving his room, and the little Duke slept in peace under the great feathered canopy in the Royal Bedchamber, and dreamed of Virginia.

## V.

A few days after this, Virginia and her curly-haired cavalier went out riding on Brockley meadows, where she tore her habit so badly in getting through a hedge, that, on their return home, she made up her mind to go up by the back staircase so as not to be seen. As she was running past the Tapestry Chamber, the door of which happened to be open, she fancied she saw some one inside, and thinking it was her mother's maid, who sometimes used to bring her work there, looked in to ask her to mend her habit. To her immense surprise, however, it was the Canterville Ghost himself! He was sitting by the window, watching the ruined gold of the yellowing trees fly through the air, and the red leaves dancing madly down the long avenue. His head was leaning on his hand,

127

and his whole attitude was one of extreme depression. Indeed, so forlorn, and so much out of repair did he look, that little Virginia, whose first idea had been to run away and lock herself in her room, was filled with pity, and determined to try and comfort him. So light was her footfall, and so deep his melancholy, that he was not aware of her presence till she spoke to him.

"I am so sorry for you," she said, "but my brothers are going back to Eton to-morrow, and then, if you behave yourself, no one will annoy you."

"It is absurd asking me to behave myself," he answered, looking round in astonishment at the pretty little girl who had ventured to address him, "quite absurd. I must rattle my chains, and groan through keyholes, and walk about at night, if that is what you mean. It is my only reason for existing."

"It is no reason at all for existing, and you know you have been very wicked. Mrs. Umney told us, the first day we arrived here, that you had killed your wife."

"Well, I quite admit it," said the Ghost petulantly, "but it was a purely family matter, and concerned no one else."

"It is very wrong to kill any one," said Virginia, who at times had a sweet Puritan gravity, caught from some old New England ancestor.

"Oh, I hate the cheap severity of abstract ethics! My wife was very plain, never had my ruffs properly starched, and knew nothing about cookery. Why, there was a buck I had shot in Hogley Woods, a magnificent pricket, and do you know how she had it sent up to table? However, it is no matter now, for it is all over, and I don't think it was very nice of her brothers to starve me to death, though I did kill her."

"Starve you to death? Oh, Mr. Ghost, I mean Sir Simon, are you hungry? I have a sandwich in my case. Would you like it?"

"No, thank you, I never eat anything now; but it is very kind of you, all the same, and you are much nicer than the rest of your horrid, rude, vulgar, dishonest family."

"Stop!" cried Virginia stamping her foot, "it is you who are rude, and horrid, and vulgar, and as for dishonesty, you know you stole the paints out of my box to try and furbish up that ridiculous blood-stain in the library. First you took all my reds, including the vermilion, and I couldn't do any more sunsets, then you took the emerald-green and the chrome-yellow, and finally I had nothing left but indigo and Chinese white, and could only do moonlight scenes, which are always depressing to look at, and not at all easy to paint. I never told on you, though I was very much annoyed, and it was most ridiculous, the whole thing; for who ever heard of emerald-green blood?"

"Well, really," said the Ghost, rather meekly, "what was I to do? It is a very difficult thing to get real blood nowadays, and, as your brother began it all with his Paragon Detergent, I certainly saw no reason why I should not have your paints. As for colour, that is always a matter of taste: the Cantervilles have blue blood, for instance, the very bluest in England; but I know you Americans don't care for things of this kind."

"You know nothing about it, and the best thing you can do is to emigrate and improve your mind. My father will be only too happy to give you a free passage, and though there is a heavy duty on spirits of every kind, there will be no difficulty about the Custom House, as the officers are all Democrats. Once in New York, you are sure to be a great success. I know lots of people there who would give a hundred thousand dollars to have a grandfather, and much more than that to have a family ghost."

"I don't think I should like America."

"I suppose because we have no ruins and no curiosities," said Virginia satirically.

"No ruins! no curiosities!" answered the Ghost; "you have your navy and your manners."

"Good evening; I will go and ask papa to get the twins an extra week's holiday."

"Please don't go, Miss Virginia," he cried; "I am so lonely and so unhappy, and I really don't know what to do. I want to go to sleep and I cannot."

"That's quite absurd! You have merely to go to bed and blow out the candle. It is very difficult sometimes to keep awake, especially at church, but there is no difficulty at all about sleeping. Why, even babies know how to do that, and they are not very clever."

"I have not slept for three hundred years," he said sadly, and Virginia's beautiful blue eyes opened in wonder; "for three hundred years I have not slept, and I am so tired."

Virginia grew quite grave, and her little lips trembled like rose-leaves. She came towards him, and kneeling down at his side, looked up into his old withered face.

"Poor, poor Ghost," she murmured; "have you no place where you can sleep?"

"Far away beyond the pinewoods," he answered, in a low dreamy voice, "there is a little garden. There the grass grows long and deep, there are the great white stars of the hemlock flower, there the nightingale sings all night long. All night long he sings, and the cold, crystal moon looks down, and the yew-tree spreads out its giant arms over the sleepers."

Virginia's eyes grew dim with tears, and she hid her face in her hands.

"You mean the Garden of Death," she whispered.

"Yes, Death. Death must be so beautiful. To lie in the soft brown earth, with the grasses waving above one's head, and listen to silence. To have no yesterday, and no to-morrow. To forget time, to forgive life, to be at peace. You can help me. You can open for me the portals of Death's house, for Love is always with you, and Love is stronger than Death is."

Virginia trembled, a cold shudder ran through her, and for a few moments there was silence. She felt as if she was in a terrible dream.

Then the Ghost spoke again, and his voice sounded like the sighing of the wind.

"Have you ever read the old prophecy on the library window?"

"Oh, often," cried the little girl, looking up; "I know it quite well. It is painted in curious black letters, and is difficult to read. There are only six lines:

> When a golden girl can win
> Prayer from out the lips of sin,
> When the barren almond bears,
> And a little child gives away its tears,
> Then shall all the house be still
> And peace come to Canterville.

But I don't know what they mean.

"They mean," he said sadly, "that you must weep with me for my sins, because I have no tears, and pray with me for my soul, because I have no faith, and then, if you have always been sweet, and good, and gentle, the Angel of Death will have mercy on me. You will see fearful shapes in darkness and wicked voices will whisper in your ear, but they will not harm you, for against the purity of a little child the powers of Hell cannot prevail.''

Virginia made no answer, and the Ghost wrung his hands in wild despair as he looked down at her bowed golden head. Suddenly she stood up, very pale, and with a strange light in her eyes. "I am not afraid," she said, firmly, "and I will ask the Angel to have mercy on you."

He rose from his seat with a faint cry of joy, and taking her hand bent over it with old-fashioned grace and kissed it. His fingers were as cold as ice, and his lips burned like fire, but Virginia did not falter, as he led her across the dusky room. On the faded green tapestry were broidered little huntsmen. They blew their tasselled horns and with their tiny hands waved to her to go back. "Go back! little Virginia," they cried, "go back!" but the Ghost clutched her hand more tightly, and she shut her eyes against them. Horrible animals with lizard

tails, and goggle eyes, blinked at her from the
carven chimney-piece, and murmured "Beware!
little Virginia, beware! we may never see you
again," but the Ghost glided on more swiftly,
and Virginia did not listen. When they
reached the end of the room he stopped, and
muttered some words she could not understand.
She opened her eyes, and saw the wall slowly
fading away like a mist, and a great black cav-
ern in front of her. A bitter cold wind swept
round them, and she felt something pulling at
her dress. "Quick, quick," cried the Ghost, "or
it will be too late," and, in a moment, the wainscoting had closed behind them, and the Tapestry
Chamber was empty.

# VI.

About ten minutes later, the bell rang for
tea, and, as Virginia did not come down, Mrs.
Otis sent up one of the footmen to tell her.
After a little time he returned and said that he
could not find Miss Virginia anywhere. As she
was in the habit of going out to the garden
every evening to get flowers for the dinner-table,
Mrs. Otis was not at all alarmed at first, but
when six o'clock struck, and Virginia did not
appear, she became really agitated, and sent the
boys out to look for her, while she herself and
Mr. Otis searched every room in the house. At
half-past six the boys came back and said that
they could find no trace of their sister anywhere.
They were all now in the greatest state of excitement, and did not know what to do, when
Mr. Otis suddenly remembered that, some few

days before, he had given a band of gipsies permission to camp in the park. He accordingly at once set off for Blackfell Hollow, where he knew they were, accompanied by his eldest son and two of the farm-servants. The little Duke of Cheshire, who was perfectly frantic with anxiety, begged hard to be allowed to go too, but Mr. Otis would not allow him, as he was afraid there might be a scuffle. On arriving at the spot, however, he found that the gipsies had gone, and it was evident that their departure had been rather sudden, as the fire was still burning, and some plates were lying on the grass. Having sent off Washington and the two men to scour the district, he ran home, and despatched telegrams to all the police inspectors in the county, telling them to look out for a little girl who had been kidnapped by tramps or gipsies. He then ordered his horse to be brought round, and, after insisting on his wife and the three boys sitting down to dinner, rode off down the Ascot road with a groom. He had hardly, however, gone a couple of miles, when he heard somebody galloping after him, and, looking round, saw the little Duke coming up on his pony, with his face very flushed and no hat.

"I'm awfully sorry, Mr. Otis," gasped out the boy, "but I can't eat any dinner as long as Virginia is lost. Please don't be angry with me; if you had let us be engaged last year, there would never have been all this trouble. You won't send me back, will you? I can't go! I won't go!"

The Minister could not help smiling at the handsome young scapegrace, and was a good deal touched at his devotion to Virginia, so leaning down from his horse, he patted him kindly. on the shoulders, and said, "Well, Cecil, if you won't go back I suppose you must come with me, but I must get you a hat at Ascot."

"Oh, bother my hat! I want Virginia!" cried the little Duke, laughing, and they galloped on to the railway station. There Mr. Otis inquired of the station-master if any one answering to the description of Virginia had been seen on the platform, but could get no news of her. The station-master, however, wired up and down the line, and assured him that a strict watch would be kept for her, and, after having bought a hat for the little Duke from a linen-draper, who was just putting up his shutters, Mr. Otis rode off to Bexley, a village about four miles away, which he was told was a well-known haunt of the gipsies, as there was a large common next to it. Here they roused up the rural policeman, but could get no information from him, and, after riding all over the common, they turned their horses' heads homewards, and reached the Chase about eleven o'clock, dead-tired and almost heart-broken. They found Washington and the twins waiting for them at the gate-house with lanterns, as the avenue was very dark. Not the slightest trace of Virginia had been discovered. The gipsies had been caught on Brockley meadows, but she was not with them, and they had explained their sudden departure by saying that they had mistaken the date of Chorton Fair, and had gone off in a hurry for fear they might be late. Indeed, they had been quite distressed at hearing of Virginia's disappearance, as they were very grateful to Mr. Otis for having allowed them to camp in his park, and four of their number had stayed behind to help in the search. The carp-pond had been dragged, and the whole Chase thoroughly gone over, but without any result. It was evident that, for that night at any rate, Virginia was lost to them; and it was

in a state of the deepest depression that Mr.
Otis and the boys walked up to the house, the
groom following behind with the two horses and
the pony. In the hall they found a group of
frightened servants, and lying on a sofa in the
library was poor Mrs. Otis, almost out of her
mind with terror and anxiety, and having her
forehead bathed with eau-de-cologne by the old
housekeeper. Mr. Otis at once insisted on her
having something to eat, and ordered up supper
for the whole party. It was a melancholy meal,
as hardly any one spoke, and even the twins
were awestruck and subdued, as they were very
fond of their sister. When they had finished,
Mr. Otis, in spite of the entreaties of the little
Duke, ordered them all to bed, saying that nothing more could be done that night, and that he
would telegraph in the morning to Scotland
Yard for some detectives to be sent down immediately. Just as they were passing out of the
dining-room, midnight began to boom from the
clock tower, and when the last stroke sounded
they heard a crash and a sudden shrill cry; a
dreadful peal of thunder shook the house, a
strain of unearthly music floated through the
air, a panel at the top of the staircase flew back

with a loud noise, and out on the landing, looking very pale and white, with a little casket in her hand, stepped Virginia. In a moment they had all rushed up to her. Mrs. Otis clasped her passionately in her arms, the Duke smothered her with violent kisses, and the twins executed a wild war-dance round the group.

"Good heavens! child, where have you been?" said Mr. Otis, rather angrily, thinking that she had been playing some foolish trick on them. "Cecil and I have been riding all over the country looking for you, and your mother has been frightened to death. You must never play these practical jokes any more."

"Except on the Ghost! except on the Ghost!" shrieked the twins, as they capered about.

"My own darling, thank God you are found; you must never leave my side again," murmured Mrs. Otis, as she kissed the trembling child, and smoothed the tangled gold of her hair.

"Papa," said Virginia quietly, "I have been with the Ghost. He is dead, and you must come and see him. He had been very wicked, but he was really sorry for all that he had done, and

he gave me this box of beautiful jewels before
he died.''

The whole family gazed at her in mute amazement, but she was quite grave and serious; and,
turning round, she led them through the open-
ing in the wainscoting down a narrow secret
corridor, Washington following with a lighted
candle, which he had caught up from the table.
Finally, they came to a great oak door, studded
with rusty nails. When Virginia touched it, it
swung back on its heavy hinges, and they found
themselves in a little low room, with a vaulted
ceiling, and one tiny grated window. Imbedded
in the wall was a huge iron ring, and chained
to it was a gaunt skeleton, that was stretched
out at full length on the stone floor, and seemed
to be trying to grasp with its long fleshless
fingers an old-fashioned trencher and ewer, that
were placed just out of its reach. The jug had
evidently been once filled with water, as it was
covered inside with green mould. There was
nothing on the trencher but a pile of dust.
Virginia knelt down beside the skeleton, and,
folding her little hands together, began to pray
silently, while the rest of the party looked on

in wonder at the terrible tragedy whose secret was now disclosed to them.

"Hallo!" suddenly exclaimed one of the twins, who had been looking out of the window to try and discover in what wing of the house the room was situated. "Hallo! the old withered almond-tree has blossomed. I can see the flowers quite plainly in the moonlight."

"God has forgiven him," said Virginia gravely, as she rose to her feet, and a beautiful light seemed to illumine her face.

"What an angel you are!" cried the young Duke, and he put his arm round her neck, and kissed her.

# VII.

Four days after these curious incidents a
funeral started from Canterville Chase at about
eleven o'clock at night. The hearse was drawn
by eight black horses, each of which carried on
its head a great tuft of nodding ostrich-plumes,
and the leaden coffin was covered by a rich purple pall, on which was embroidered in gold the
Canterville coat-of-arms. By the side of the
hearse and the coaches walked the servants with
lighted torches, and the whole procession was
wonderfully impressive. Lord Canterville was
the chief mourner, having come up specially
from Wales to attend the funeral, and sat in
the first carriage along with little Virginia.
Then came the United States Minister and his
wife, then Washington and the three boys, and
in the last carriage was Mrs. Umney. It was
generally felt that, as she had been frightened

by the ghost for more than fifty years of her life, she had a right to see the last of him. A deep grave had been dug in the corner of the churchyard, just under the old yew-tree, and the service was read in the most impressive manner by the Rev. Augustus Dampier. When the ceremony was over, the servants, according to an old custom observed in the Canterville family, extinguished their torches, and, as the coffin was being lowered into the grave, Virginia stepped forward, and laid on it a large cross made of white and pink almond-blossoms. As she did so, the moon came out from behind a cloud, and flooded with its silent silver the little churchyard, and from a distant copse a nightingale began to sing. She thought of the ghost's description of the Garden of Death, her eyes became dim with tears, and she hardly spoke a word during the drive home.

The next morning, before Lord Canterville went up to town, Mr. Otis had an interview with him on the subject of the jewels the ghost had given to Virginia. They were perfectly magnificent, especially a certain ruby necklace with old Venetian setting, which was really a superb specimen of sixteenth-century work, and their value was so great that Mr. Otis felt considerable scruples about allowing his daughter to accept them.

"My lord," he said, "I know that in this country mortmain is held to apply to trinkets as well as to land, and it is quite clear to me that these jewels are, or should be, heirlooms in your family. I must beg you, accordingly, to take them to London with you, and to regard them simply as a portion of your property which has been restored to you under certain strange conditions. As for my daughter, she is merely a child, and has as yet, I am glad to say, but little interest in such appurtenances of idle luxury. I am also informed by Mrs. Otis, who, I may say, is no mean authority upon Art— having had the privilege of spending several winters in Boston when she was a girl—that these gems are of great monetary worth, and if offered for sale would fetch a tall price. Under these circumstances, Lord Canterville, I feel sure that you will recognise how impossible it would be for me to allow them to remain in the possession of any member of my family; and, indeed, all such vain gauds and toys, however suitable or necessary to the dignity of the British aristocracy, would be completely out of place among those who have been brought up on the severe, and I believe immortal, principles of Republican simplicity. Perhaps I should mention that Virginia is very anxious that you should allow her to retain the box, as a memento of your unfortunate but misguided ancestor. As it is extremely old, and consequently a good deal out of repair, you may perhaps think fit to comply with her request. For my own part, I confess I am a good deal surprised to find a child of mine expressing sympathy with mediæ-valism in any form, and can only account for it by the fact that Virginia was born in one of your London suburbs shortly after Mrs. Otis had returned from a trip to Athens.''

Lord Canterville listened very gravely to the worthy Minister's speech, pulling his grey moustache now and then to hide an involuntary smile, and when Mr. Otis had ended, he shook him cordially by the hands, and said, ''My dear sir, your charming little daughter rendered my unlucky ancestor, Sir Simon, a very important service, and I and my family are much indebted to her for her marvellous courage and pluck. The jewels are clearly hers, and, egad, I believe that

if I were heartless enough to take them from
her, the wicked old fellow would be out of his
grave in a fortnight, leading me the devil of a
life.  As for their being heirlooms, nothing is
an heirloom that is not so mentioned in a will or
legal document, and the existence of these jewels
has been quite unknown.  I assure you I have
no more claim on them than your butler, and
when Miss Virginia grows up I daresay she will
be pleased to have pretty things to wear.  Besides, you forget, Mr. Otis, that you took the
furniture and the ghost at a valuation, and anything that belonged to the ghost passed at once
into your possession, as, whatever activity Sir
Simon may have shown in the corridor at night,
in point of law he was really dead, and you acquired his property by purchase.''

Mr. Otis was a good deal distressed at Lord
Canterville's refusal, and begged him to recon-
sider his decision, but the good-natured peer
was quite firm, and finally induced the Minister
to allow his daughter to retain the present the
ghost had given her, and when, in the spring of
1890, the young Duchess of Cheshire was presented at the Queen's first drawing-room on the
occasion of her marriage, her jewels were the

universal theme of admiration. For Virginia received the coronet, which is the reward of all good little American girls, and was married to her boy-lover as soon as he came of age. They were both so charming, and they loved each other so much, that every one was delighted at the match, except the old Marchioness of Dumbleton, who had tried to catch the Duke for one of her seven unmarried daughters, and had given no less than three expensive dinner-parties for that purpose, and, strange to say, Mr. Otis himself. Mr. Otis was extremely fond of the young Duke personally, but, theoretically, he objected to titles, and, to use his own words, "was not without apprehension lest amid the enervating influences of a pleasure-loving aristocracy, the true principles of Republican simplicity should be forgotten." His objections, however, were completely overruled, and I believe that when he walked up the aisle of St. George's, Hanover Square, with his daughter leaning on his arm, there was not a prouder man in the whole length and breadth of England.

The Duke and Duchess, after the honeymoon was over, went down to Canterville Chase, and on the day after their arrival they walked over in the afternoon to the lonely churchyard by the pine-woods.  There had been a great deal of difficulty at first about the inscription on Sir Simon's tombstone, but finally it had been decided to engrave on it simply the initials of the old gentleman's name, and the verse from the library window.  The Duchess had brought with her some lovely roses, which she strewed upon the grave, and after they had stood by it for some time they strolled into the ruined chancel of the old abbey.  There the Duchess sat down on a fallen pillar, while her husband lay at her feet smoking a cigarette and looking up at her beautiful eyes.  Suddenly he threw his cigarette away, took hold of her hand, and said to her, "Virginia, a wife should have no secrets from her husband."

"Dear Cecil!  I have no secrets from you."

"Yes, you have," he answered, smiling, "you have never told me what happened to you when you were locked up with the ghost."

"I have never told any one, Cecil," said Virginia gravely.

"I know that, but you might tell me."

"Please don't ask me, Cecil, I cannot tell you. Poor Sir Simon!  I owe him a great deal.  Yes,

don't laugh, Cecil, I really do. He made me
see what Life is, and what Death signifies, and
why Love is stronger than both.''

The Duke rose and kissed his wife lovingly.

''You can have your secret as long as I have
your heart,'' he murmured.

''You have always had that, Cecil.''

''And you will tell our children some day,
won't you?''

Virginia blushed.

# The Model Millionaire.

## A Note of Admiration.

# THE MODEL MILLIONAIRE.

Unless one is wealthy there is no use in being a charming fellow. Romance is the privilege of the rich, not the profession of the unemployed. The poor should be practical and prosaic. It is better to have a permanent income than to be fascinating. These are the great truths of modern life which Hughie Erskine never realised. Poor Hughie! Intellectually, we must admit, he was not of much importance. He never said a brilliant or even an ill-natured thing in his life. But then he was wonderfully good-looking, with his crisp brown hair, his clear-cut profile, and his grey eyes. He was as popular with men as he was with women, and he had every accomplishment except that of making money. His father had bequeathed him his cavalry sword, and a *History of the Peninsular War* in fifteen volumes. Hughie hung the first over his looking-glass, put the second on a shelf between Ruff's *Guide* and Bailey's *Magazine,* and lived

155

on two hundred a year that an old aunt allowed him. He had tried everything. He had gone on the Stock Exchange for six months; but what was a butterfly to do among bulls and bears? He had been a tea-merchant for a little longer, but had soon tired of pekoe and souchong. Then he had tried selling dry sherry. That did not answer; the sherry was a little too dry. Ultimately he became nothing, a delightful, in-effectual young man with a perfect profile and no profession.

To make matters worse, he was in love. The girl he loved was Laura Merton, the daughter of a retired Colonel who had lost his temper and his digestion in India, and had never found either of them again. Laura adored him, and he was ready to kiss her shoe-strings. They were the handsomest couple in London, and had not a penny-piece between them. The Colonel was very fond of Hughie, but would not hear of any engagement.

"Come to me, my boy, when you have got ten thousand pounds of your own, and we will see about it," he used to say; and Hughie looked very glum on those days, and had to go to Laura for consolation.

One morning, as he was on his way to Holland Park, where the Mertons lived, he dropped in to see a great friend of his, Alan Trevor. Trevor was a painter. Indeed, few people escape that nowadays. But he was also an artist, and artists are rather rare. Personally he was a strange rough fellow, with a freckled face and a red ragged beard. However, when he took up the brush he was a real master, and his pictures were eagerly sought after. He had been very much attracted by Hughie at first, it must be acknowledged, entirely on account of his personal charm. "The only people a painter should know," he used to say, "are people who are *bête* and beautiful, people who are an artistic pleasure to look at and an intellectual repose to talk to. Men who are dandies and women who are darlings rule the world, at least they should do so." However, after he got to know Hughie better, he liked him quite as much for his bright buoyant spirits and his generous reckless nature, and had given him the permanent *entrée* to his studio.

When Hughie came in he found Trevor putting the finishing touches to a wonderful life-size picture of a beggar-man. The beggar himself was standing on a raised platform in a corner of the studio. He was a wizened old man, with a face like wrinkled parchment, and a most piteous expression. Over his shoulders was flung a coarse brown cloak, all tears and tatters; his thick boots were patched and cobbled, and with one hand he leant on a rough stick, while with the other he held out his battered hat for alms.

"What an amazing model!" whispered Hughie, as he shook hands with his friend.

"An amazing model?" shouted Trevor at the top of his voice; "I should think so! Such beggars as he are not to be met with every day. A *trouvaille, mon cher;* a living Velasquez! My stars! what an etching Rembrandt would have made of him!"

"Poor old chap!" said Hughie, "how miserable he looks! But I suppose, to you painters, his face is his fortune?"

"Certainly," replied Trevor, "you don't want a beggar to look happy, do you?"

"How much does a model get for sitting?" asked Hughie, as he found himself a comfortable seat on a divan.

"A shilling an hour."

"And how much do you get for your picture, Alan?"

"Oh, for this I get two thousand."

"Pounds?"

"Guineas. Painters, poets, and physicians always get guineas."

"Well, I think the model should have a percentage," cried Hughie, laughing; "they work quite as hard as you do."

"Nonsense, nonsense! Why, look at the trouble of laying on the paint alone, and standing all day long at one's easel! It's all very well, Hughie, for you to talk, but I assure you that there are moments when Art almost attains to the dignity of manual labour. But you mustn't chatter; I'm very busy. Smoke a cigarette, and keep quiet."

After some time the servant came in, and told Trevor that the frame-maker wanted to speak to him.

"Don't run away, Hughie," he said, as he went out, "I will be back in a moment."

The old beggar-man took advantage of Trevor's absence to rest for a moment on a wooden bench that was behind him. He looked so forlorn and wretched that Hughie could not help

pitying him, and felt in his pockets to see what
money he had. All he could find was a sovereign and some coppers. "Poor old fellow," he
thought to himself, "he wants it more than I do,
but it means no hansoms for a fortnight;" and
he walked across the studio and slipped the sovereign into the beggar's hand.

The old man started, and a faint smile flitted
across his withered lips. "Thank you, sir," he
said, "thank you."

Then Trevor arrived, and Hughie took his
leave, blushing a little at what he had done. He
spent the day with Laura, got a charming scolding for his extravagance, and had to walk home.

That night he strolled into the Palette Club
about eleven o'clock, and found Trevor sitting
by himself in the smoking-room drinking hock
and seltzer.

"Well, Alan, did you get the picture finished
all right?" he said, as he lit his cigarette.

"Finished and framed, my boy!" answered
Trevor; "and by-the-bye, you have made a con-
quest. That old model you saw is quite devoted
to you. I had to tell him all about you—who
you are, where you live, what your income is,
what prospects you have——"

"My dear Alan," cried Hughie, "I shall probably find him waiting for me when I go home. But of course you are only joking. Poor old wretch! I wish I could do something for him. I think it is dreadful that any one should be so miserable. I have got heaps of old clothes at home—do you think he would care for any of them? Why, his rags were falling to bits."

"But he looks splendid in them," said Trevor. "I wouldn't paint him in a frock-coat for anything. What you call rags I call romance. What seems poverty to you is picturesqueness to me. However, I'll tell him of your offer."

"Alan," said Hughie seriously, "you painters are a heartless lot."

"An artist's heart is his head," replied Trevor; "and besides, our business is to realise the world as we see it, not to reform it as we know it. *A chacun son métier.* And now tell me how Laura is. The old model was quite interested in her."

"You don't mean to say you talked to him about her?"

"Certainly I did. He knows all about the relentless colonel, the lovely Laura, and the £10,000.''

''You told that old beggar all my private affairs?'' cried Hughie, looking very red and angry.

''My dear boy,'' said Trevor, smiling, ''that old beggar, as you call him, is one of the richest men in Europe. He could buy all London to-morrow without overdrawing his account. He has a house in every capital, dines off gold plate, and can prevent Russia going to war when he chooses.''

''What on earth do you mean?'' exclaimed Hughie.

''What I say,'' said Trevor. ''The old man you saw to-day in the studio was Baron Haus-berg. He is a great friend of mine, buys all my pictures and that sort of thing, and gave me a commission a month ago to paint him as a beggar. *Que voulez-vous? La fantaisie d'un millionaire!* And I must say he made a mag-nificent figure in his rags, or perhaps I should say in my rags; they are an old suit I got in Spain.''

''Baron Hausberg!'' cried Hughie. ''Good

heavens! I gave him a sovereign!'' and he sank into an armchair the picture of dismay.

"Gave him a sovereign!'' shouted Trevor, and he burst into a roar of laughter. ''My dear boy, you'll never see it again. *Son affaire c'est l'argent des autres.*''

"I think you might have told me, Alan,'' said Hughie sulkily, "and not have let me make such a fool of myself.''

"Well, to begin with, Hughie,'' said Trevor, "it never entered my mind that you went about distributing alms in that reckless way. I can understand your kissing a pretty model, but your giving a sovereign to an ugly one—by Jove, no! Besides, the fact is that I really was not at home to-day to any one; and when you came in I didn't know whether Hausberg would like his name mentioned. You know he wasn't in full dress.''

"What a duffer he must think me!'' said Hughie.

"Not at all. He was in the highest spirits after you left; kept chuckling to himself and rubbing his old wrinkled hands together. I couldn't make out why he was so interested to know all about you; but I see it all now. He'll invest your sovereign for you, Hughie, pay you the interest every six months, and have a capital story to tell after dinner.''

''I am an unlucky devil,'' growled Hughie. ''The best thing I can do is to go to bed; and, my dear Alan, you musn't tell any one. I shouldn't dare show my face in the Row.''

''Nonsense! It reflects the highest credit on your philanthropic spirit, Hughie. And don't run away. Have another cigarette, and you can talk about Laura as much as you like.''

However, Hughie wouldn't stop, but walked home, feeling very unhappy and leaving Alan Trevor in fits of laughter.

The next morning, as he was at breakfast, the servant brought him up a card on which was written, ''Monsieur Gustave Naudin, *de la part de* M. le Baron Hausberg.'' ''I suppose he has come for an apology,'' said Hughie to himself; and he told the servant to show the visitor up.

An old gentleman with gold spectacles and grey hair came into the room, and said, in a slight French accent, ''Have I the honour of addressing Monsieur Erskine?''

Hughie bowed.

"I have come from Baron Hausberg," he continued. "The Baron——"

"I beg, sir, that you will offer him my sincerest apologies," stammered Hughie.

"The Baron," said the old gentleman, with a smile, "has commissioned me to bring you this letter;" and he extended a sealed envelope.

On the outside was written, "A wedding present to Hugh Erskine and Laura Merton, from an old beggar," and inside was a cheque for £10,000.

When they were married Alan Trevor was the best man, and the Baron made a speech at the wedding-breakfast.

"Millionaire models," remarked Alan, "are rare enough; but by Jove, model millionaires are rarer still!"

# The Portrait of Mr. W. H.

# THE PORTRAIT OF MR. W. H.

## I.

I had been dining with Erskine in his pretty little house in Birdcage Walk, and we were sitting in the library over our coffee and cigarettes, when the question of literary forgeries happened to turn up in conversation. I cannot at present remember how it was that we struck upon this somewhat curious topic, as it was at that time, but I know that we had a long discussion about Macpherson, Ireland, and Chatterton, and that with regard to the last I insisted that his so-called forgeries were merely the result of an artistic desire for perfect representation; that we had no right to quarrel with an artist for the conditions under which he chooses to present his work: and that all Art being to a certain degree a mode of acting, an attempt to realise one's own personality on some imaginative plane out of reach of the trammelling accidents and limitations of real life, to censure an artist for a forgery was to confuse an ethical with an æsthetical problem.

Erskine, who was a good deal older than I was, and had been listening to me with the amused deference of a man of forty, suddenly put his hand upon my shoulder and said to me, "What would you say about a young man who had a strange theory about a certain work of art, believed in his theory, and committed a forgery in order to prove it?"

"Ah! that is quite a different matter," I answered.

Erskine remained silent for a few moments, looking at the thin grey threads of smoke that were rising from his cigarette. "Yes," he said, after a pause, "quite different."

There was something in the tone of his voice, a slight touch of bitterness perhaps, that excited my curiosity. "Did you ever know anybody who did that?" I cried.

"Yes," he answered, throwing his cigarette into the fire,—"a great friend of mine, Cyril Graham. He was very fascinating, and very foolish, and very heartless. However, he left me the only legacy I ever received in my life."

"What was that?" I exclaimed. Erskine rose from his seat, and going over to a tall inlaid cabinet that stood between the two windows, unlocked it, and came back to where I was sitting, holding in his hand a small panel picture set in an old and somewhat tarnished Elizabethan frame.

It was the full-length portrait of a young man in late sixteenth-century costume, standing by a table, with his right hand resting on an open book. He seemed about seventeen years of age, and was of quite extraordinary personal beauty, though evidently somewhat effeminate. Indeed, had it not been for the dress and the closely cropped hair, one would have said that the face, with its dreamy wistful eyes, and its delicate scarlet lips, was the face of a girl. In manner, and especially in the treatment of the hands, the picture reminded one of François Clouet's later work. The black velvet doublet with its fantastically gilded points, and the peacock-blue back-ground against which it showed up so pleasantly, and from which it gained such luminous value of colour, were quite in Clouet's style; and the two masks of Tragedy and Comedy that hung somewhat formally from the marble pedestal had that hard severity of touch —so different from the facile grace of the Italians—which even at the Court of France the great Flemish master, never completely lost, and which in itself has always been a characteristic of the northern temper.

"It is a charming thing," I cried; "but who is this wonderful young man, whose beauty Art has so happily preserved for us?"

"This is the portrait of Mr. W. H.," said Erskine, with a sad smile. It might have been a chance effect of light, but it seemed to me that his eyes were quite bright with tears.

"Mr. W. H.!" I exclaimed; "who was Mr. W. H.?"

"Don't you remember?" he answered; "look at the book on which his hand is resting."

"I see there is some writing there, but I cannot make it out," I replied.

"Take this magnifying glass and try," said Erskine, with the same sad smile still playing about his mouth.

I took the glass, and moving the lamp a little

nearer, I began to spell out the crabbed six-teenth-century handwriting. "To the onlie be-getter of these insuing sonnets." . . . . "Good heavens!" I cried, "is this Shakespeare's Mr. W. H.?"

"Cyril Graham used to say so," muttered Erskine.

"But it is not a bit like Lord Pembroke," I answered. "I know the Penshurst portraits very well. I was staying near there a few weeks ago."

"Do you really believe then that the Sonnets are addressed to Lord Pembroke?" he asked.

"I am sure of it," I answered. "Pembroke, Shakespeare, and Mrs. Mary Fitton are the three personages of the Sonnets; there is no doubt at all about it."

"Well, I agree with you," said Erskine, "but I did not always think so. I used to believe—well, I suppose I used to believe in Cyril Graham and his theory."

"And what was that?" I asked, looking at the wonderful portrait, which had already be-gun to have a strange fascination for me.

"It is a long story," said Erskine, taking the picture away from me—rather abruptly I thought at the time—"a very long story, but if you care to hear it, I will tell it to you."

"I love theories about the Sonnets," I cried; "but I don't think I am likely to be converted to any new idea. The matter has ceased to be a mystery to any one. Indeed, I wonder that it ever was a mystery."

"As I don't believe in the theory, I am not likely to convert you to it," said Erskine, laughing, "but it may interest you."

"Tell it to me, of course," I answered. "If it is half as delightful as the picture, I shall be more than satisfied."

"Well," said Erskine, lighting a cigarette, "I must begin by telling you about Cyril Graham himself. He and I were at the same house at Eton. I was a year or two older than he was, but we were immense friends, and did all our work and all our play together. There was, of course, a good deal more play than work, but I cannot say that I am sorry for that. It is always an advantage not to have received a sound commercial education, and what I learned in the playing fields at Eton has been quite as useful to me as anything I was taught at Cambridge. I should tell you that Cyril's

father and mother were both dead. They had
been drowned in a horrible yachting accident off
the Isle of Wight. His father had been in the
diplomatic service, and had married a daughter,
the only daughter, in fact, of old Lord Crediton,
who became Cyril's guardian after the death of
his parents. I don't think that Lord Crediton
cared very much for Cyril. He had never
really forgiven his daughter for marrying a
man who had no title. He was an extraordinary old aristocrat, who swore like a coster-
monger, and had the manners of a farmer. I
remember seeing him once on Speech-day. He
growled at me, gave me a sovereign, and told
me not to grow up "a damned Radical" like my
father. Cyril had very little affection for him,
and was only too glad to spend most of his holidays with us in Scotland.. They never really
got on together at all. Cyril thought him a bear.
and he thought Cyril effeminate. He was effeminate, I suppose, in some things, though he
was a very good rider and a capital fencer. In
fact he got the foils before he left Eton. But
he was very languid in his manner, and not a
little vain of his good looks, and had a strong
objection to football. The two things that

really gave him pleasure were poetry and acting.
At Eton he was always dressing up and reciting
Shakespeare, and when we went up to Trinity
he became a member of the A.D.C. his first term.
I remember I was always very jealous of his acting. I was absurdly devoted to him; I suppose
because we were so different in some things. I
was a rather awkward, weakly lad, with huge
feet and horribly freckled. Freckles run in
Scotch families just as gout does in English
families. Cyril used to say that of the two he
preferred the gout; but he always set an absurdly high value on personal appearance, and once
read a paper before our debating society to
prove that it was better to be good-looking than
to be good. He certainly was wonderfully
handsome. People who did not like him, Phil-
istines and college tutors, and young men reading for the Church used to say that he was
merely pretty; but there was a great deal more
in his face than mere prettiness. I think he was
the most splendid creature I ever saw, and
nothing could exceed the grace of his movements, the charm of his manner. He fascinated
everybody who was worth fascinating, and a
great many people who were not. He was often

wilful and petulant, and I used to think him
dreadfully insincere.  It was due, I think, chief-
ly to his inordinate desire to please.  Poor
Cyril!  I told him once that he was contented
with very cheap triumphs, but he only laughed.
He was horribly spoiled.  All charming people
I fancy, are spoiled.  It is the secret of their
attraction.

"However, I must tell you about Cyril's acting.  You know that no actresses are allowed
to play at the A.D.C.  At least they were not
in my time.  I don't know how it is now.  Well,
of course, Cyril was always cast for the girls'
parts, and when 'As You Like It' was produced
he played Rosalind.  It was a marvellous performance.  In fact, Cyril Graham was the only
perfect Rosalind I have ever seen.  It would
be impossible to describe to you the beauty, the
delicacy, the refinement of the whole thing.  It
made an immense sensation, and the horrid little theatre, as it was then, was crowded every
night.  Even when I read the play now I can't
help thinking of Cyril.  It might have been
written for him.  The next term he took his
degree, and came to London to read for the

diplomatic. But he never did any work. He spent his days in reading Shakespeare's Sonnets and his evenings at the theatre. He was, of course, wild to go on the stage. It was all that I and Lord Crediton could do to prevent him. Perhaps if he had gone on the stage he would be alive now. It is always a silly thing to give advice, but to give good advice is absolutely fatal. I hope you will never fall into that error. If you do, you will be sorry for it.

"Well, to come to the real point of the story, one day I got a letter from Cyril asking me to come round to his rooms that evening. He had charming chambers in Picadilly, overlooking the Green Park, and as I used to go to see him every day, I was rather surprised at his taking the trouble to write. Of course I went, and when I arrived I found him in a state of great excitement. He told me that he had at last discovered the true secret of Shakespeare's Sonnets; that all the scholars and critics had been entirely on the wrong tack; and that he was the first who, working purely by internal evidence, had found out who Mr. W. H. really was. He was perfectly wild with delight, and for a long time would not tell me his theory. Finally, he produced a bundle of notes, took his copy of the Sonnets off the mantelpiece, and sat down and gave me a long lecture on the whole subject.

"He began by pointing out that the young man to whom Shakespeare addressed these strangely passionate poems must have been somebody who was a really vital factor in the development of his dramatic art, and that this could not be said either of Lord Pembroke or Lord Southampton. Indeed, whoever he was, he could not have been anybody of high birth, as was shown very clearly by the 25th Sonnet, in which Shakespeare contrasts himself with those who are 'great princes' favourites;' says quite frankly—

> "'Let those who are in favour with their stars
> Of public honour and proud titles boast,
> Whilst I, whom fortune of such triumph bars,
> Unlooked for joy in that I honour most;'

and ends the sonnet by congratulating himself on the mean state of him he so adored:

> "'Then happy I, that loved and am beloved
> Where I may not remove nor be removed.'

This sonnet Cyril declared would be quite unintelligible if we fancied that it was addressed
to either the Earl of Pembroke or the Earl of
Southampton, both of whom were men of the
highest position in England and fully entitled
to be called 'great princes'; and he in corroboration of his view read me Sonnets cxxiv. and
cxxv., in which Shakespeare tells us that his
love is not 'the child of state,' that it 'suffers
not in smiling pomp,' but is 'builded far from
accident.' I listened with a good deal of interest, for I don't think the point had ever been
made before: but what followed was still more
curious, and seemed to me at the time to entirely dispose of Pembroke's claim. We know
from Meres that the Sonnets had been written
before 1598, and Sonnet civ. informs us that
Shakespeare's friendship for Mr. W. H. had
been already in existence for three years. Now
Lord Pembroke, who was born in 1580, did not
come to London till he was eighteen years of
age, that is to say till 1598, and Shakespeare's acquaintance with Mr. W. H. must
have begun in 1594, or at the latest in 1595.
Shakespeare, accordingly, could not have known

Lord Pembroke till after the Sonnets had been written.

"Cyril pointed out also that Pembroke's father did not die till 1601; whereas it was evident from the line,

'You had a father, let your son say so,'

that the father of Mr. W. H. was dead in 1598. Besides, it was absurd to imagine that any publisher of the time, and the preface is from the publisher's hand, would have ventured to address William Herbert, Earl of Pembroke, as Mr. W. H.; the case of Lord Buckhurst being spoken of as Mr. Sackville being not really a parallel instance, as Lord Buckhurst was not a peer, but merely the younger son of a peer, with a courtesy title, and the passage in 'England's Parnassus,' where he is so spoken of, is not a formal and stately dedication, but simply a casual allusion. So far for Lord Pembroke, whose supposed claims Cyril easily demolished while I sat by in wonder. With Lord Southampton Cyril had even less difficulty. Southampton became at a very early age the lover of Elizabeth Vernon, so he needed no entreaties to marry: he was not beautiful; he did not resemble his mother, as Mr. W. H. did—

> "'Thou art thy mother's glass, and she in thee
> Calls back the lovely April of her prime;'

and, above all, his Christian name was Henry, whereas the punning sonnets (cxxxv. and cxliii.) show that the Christian name of Shakespeare's friend was the same as his own—*Will*.

"As for the other suggestions of unfortunate commentators, that Mr. W. H. is a misprint for Mr. W. S., meaning Mr. William Shakespeare; that 'Mr. W. II. all, should be read 'Mr. W. Hall'; that Mr. W. H. is Mr. William Hathaway; and that a full stop should be placed after 'wisheth,' making Mr. W. H. the writer and not the subject of the dedication,—Cyril got rid of them in a very short time; and it is not worth while to mention his reasons, though I remember he sent me off into a fit of laughter by reading to me, I am glad to say not in the original, some extracts from a German commentator called Barnstorff, who insisted that Mr. W. H. was no less a person than 'Mr. William Himself.' Nor would he allow for a moment that the Sonnets are mere satires on the work of Drayton and John Davies of Hereford. To him, as indeed to me, they were poems of serious and tragic import, wrung out of the bitterness of Shakespeare's heart, and made sweet by the honey of his lips. Still less would he admit that they were merely a philosophical allegory, and that in them Shakespeare is addressing his Ideal Self, or Ideal Manhood, or the Spirit of Beauty, or the Reason, or the Divine Logos, or the Catholic Church. He felt, as indeed I think we all must feel, that the Sonnets are addressed to an individual,—to a particular young man whose personality for some reason seems to have filled the soul of Shakespeare with terrible joy and no less terrible despair.

"Having in this manner cleared the way as it were, Cyril asked me to dismiss from my mind any preconceived ideas I might have formed on the subject, and to give a fair and unbiassed hearing to his own theory. The problem he pointed out was this: Who was that young man of Shakespeare's day who, without being of noble birth or even of noble nature, was addressed by him in terms of such

passionate adoration that we can but wonder
at the strange worship, and are almost afraid
to turn the key that unlocks the mystery of
the poet's heart? Who was he whose physical
beauty was such that it became the very
corner-stone of Shakespeare's art; the very
source of Shakespeare's inspiration; the very
incarnation of Shakespeare's dreams? To look
upon him as simply the object of certain love-
poems is to miss the whole meaning of the
poems: for the art of which Shakespeare talks
in the Sonnets is not the art of the Sonnets
themselves, which indeed were to him but slight
and secret things—it is the art of the dramatist
to which he is always alluding; and he to
whom Shakespeare said—

> " ' Thou art all my art, and dost advance
>     As high as learning my rude ignorance,'—

he to whom he promised immortality,

> " ' Where breath most breathes, even in the mouth of
>     men,'—

was surely none other than the boy-actor for
whom he created Viola and Imogen, Juliet and

Rosalind, Portia and Desdemona, and Cleopatra herself.  This was Cyril Graham's theory,
evolved as you see purely from the Sonnets
themselves, and depending for its acceptance
not so much on demonstrable proof or formal
evidence, but on a kind of spiritual and artistic
sense, by which alone he claimed could the true
meaning of the poems be discerned.  I remember his reading to me that fine sonnet—

> " ' How can my Muse want subject to invent,
>     While thou dost breathe, that pour'st into my verse
>     Thine own sweet argument, too excellent
>     For every vulgar paper to rehearse?
>     O, give thyself the thanks, if aught in me
>     Worthy perusal stand against thy sight;
>     For who's so dumb that cannot write to thee,
>     When thou thyself dost give invention light?
>     Be thou the tenth Muse, ten times more in worth
>     Than those old nine which rhymers invocate;
>     And he that calls on thee, let him bring forth
>     Eternal numbers to outlive long date '

—and pointing out how completely it corrobo-
rated his theory; and indeed he went through
all the Sonnets carefully, and showed, or fancied
that he showed, that, according to his new explanation of their meaning, things that had
seemed obscure, or evil, or exaggerated, became

clear and rational, and of high artistic import, illustrating Shakespeare's conception of the true relations between the art of the actor and the art of the dramatist.

"It is of course evident that there must have been in Shakespeare's company some wonderful boy-actor of great beauty, to whom he intrusted the presentation of his noble heroines; for Shakespeare was a practical theatrical manager as well as an imaginative poet, and Cyril Graham had actually discovered the boy-actor's name. He was Will, or, as he preferred to call him, Willie Hughes. The Christian name he found of course in the punning sonnets, cxxxv. and cxliii.; the surname was, according to him, hidden in the eighth line of the 20th Sonnet, where Mr. W. H. is described as—

"'A man in hew, all *Hews* in his controwling.'

"In the original edition of the Sonnets 'Hews' is printed with a capital letter and in italics, and this, he claimed, showed clearly that a play on words was intended, his view receiving a good deal of corroboration from those sonnets in which curious puns are made

on the words 'use' and 'usury.' Of course I
was converted at once, and Willie Hughes
became to me as real a person as Shakespeare.
The only objection I made to the theory was
that the name of Willie Hughes does not occur
in the list of the actors of Shakespeare's company as it is printed in the first folio.   Cyril,
however, pointed out that the absence of Willie
Hughes's name from this list really corrobo-
rated the theory, as it was evident from
Sonnet lxxxvi. that Willie Hughes had abandoned Shakespeare's company to play at a rival
theatre, probably in some of Chapman's plays.
It is in reference to this that in the great sonnet
on Chapman Shakespeare said to Willie
Hughes—

> "'But when your countenance filled up his line,
>   Then lacked I matter; that enfeebled mine'—

the expression 'when your countenance filled
up his line' referring obviously to the beauty
of the young actor giving life and reality and
added charm to Chapman's verse, the same idea
being also put forward in the 79th Sonnet—

" ' Whilst I alone did call upon thy aid,
　My verse alone had all thy gentle grace,
　But now my gracious numbers are decayed,
　And my sick Muse does give another place; '

and in the immediately preceding sonnet, where
Shakespeare says,

" ' Every alien pen has got my *use*
　And under thee their poesy disperse,'

the play upon words (use equals Hughes) being
of course obvious, and the phrase 'under thee
their poesy disperse,' meaning 'by your assistance as an actor bring their plays before the
people.'

"It was a wonderful evening, and we sat up
almost till dawn reading and re-reading the
Sonnets. After some time, however, I began
to see that before the theory could be placed
before the world in a really perfected form, it
was necessary to get some independent evidence about the existence of this young actor
Willie Hughes. If this could be once estab-
lished, there could be no possible doubt about
his identity with Mr. W. H.; but otherwise
the theory would fall to the ground. I put
this forward very strongly to Cyril, who was

a good deal annoyed at what he called my Phi-
listine tone of mind, and indeed was rather
bitter upon the subject.  However, I made him
promise that in his own interest he would not
publish his discovery till he had put the whole
matter beyond the reach of doubt; and for
weeks and weeks we searched the registers of
City churches, the Alleyn MSS. at Dulwich,
the Record Office, the papers of the Lord Cham-
berlain—everything, in fact, that we thought
might contain some allusion to Willie Hughes.
We discovered nothing, of course, and every day
the existence of Willie Hughes seemed to me
to become more problematical.  Cyril was in a
dreadful state, and used to go over the whole
question day after day, entreating me to believe;
but I saw the one flaw in the theory, and I refused to be convinced till the actual existence
of Willie Hughes, a boy-actor of Elizabethan
days, had been placed beyond the reach of doubt
or cavil.

"One day Cyril left town to stay with his
grandfather, I thought at the time, but I afterwards heard from Lord Crediton that this was
not the case; and about a fortnight afterwards I
received a telegram from him, handed in at

Warwick, asking me to be sure to come and dine with him that evening at eight o'clock. When I arrived he said to me, 'The only apostle who did not deserve proof was S. Thomas, and S. Thomas was the only apostle who got it.' I asked him what he meant. He answered that he had not merely been able to establish the existence in the sixteenth century of a boy-actor of the name of Willie Hughes, but to prove by the most conclusive evidence that he was the Mr. W. H. of the Sonnets. He would not tell me anything more at the time; but after dinner he solemnly produced the picture I showed you, and told me that he had discovered it by the merest chance nailed to the side of an old chest that he had bought at a farmhouse in Warwickshire. The chest itself, which was a very fine example of Elizabethan work, he had, of course, brought with him, and in the centre of the front panel the initials W. H. were undoubtedly carved. It was this monogram that had attracted his attention, and he told me that it was not till he had had the chest in his possession several days that he had thought of making any careful examination of the inside. One morning, however, he saw that one of the

*'It never occurred to me that Cyril Graham
was playing a trick on me.'"*
Page 191

Warwick, asking me to be sure to come and dine with him that evening at eight o'clock. When I arrived he said to me, 'The only apostle who did not deserve proof was S. Thomas, and S. Thomas was the only apostle who got it.' I asked him what he meant. He answered that he had not merely been able to establish the existence in the sixteenth century of a boy-actor of the name of Willie Hughes, but to prove by the most conclusive evidence that he was the Mr. W. H. of the Sonnets. He would not tell me anything more at the time; but after dinner he solemnly produced the picture I showed you, and told me that he had discovered it by the merest chance nailed to the side of an old chest that he had bought at a farmhouse in Warwickshire. The chest itself, which was a very fine example of Elizabethan work, he had, of course, brought with him, and in the centre of the front panel the initials W. H. [illegible] carved. It was this monogram that [illegible] his attention, and he told me that [illegible] he had had the chest in his pos- [illegible] days that he had [illegible] of [illegible] careful examination of the inside. [illegible], however, he saw that one of the

sides of the chest was much thicker than the
other, and looking more closely, he discovered
that a framed panel picture was clamped against
it. On taking it out, he found it was the
picture that is now lying on the sofa. It was
very dirty, and covered with mould; but he
managed to clean it, and, to his great joy, saw
that he had fallen by mere chance on the one
thing for which he had been looking. Here
was an authentic portrait of Mr. W. H., with
his hand resting on the dedicatory page of the
Sonnets, and on the frame itself could be faintly
seen the name of the young man written in
black uncial letters on a faded gold ground,
'Master Will. Hews.'

"Well, what was I to say? It never occurred
to me for a moment that Cyril Graham was
playing a trick on me, or that he was trying to
prove his theory by means of a forgery."

"But is it a forgery?" I asked.

"Of course it is," said Erskine. "It is a very
good forgery; but it is a forgery none the less.
I thought at the time that Cyril was rather
calm about the whole matter; but I remember
he more than once told me that he himself required no proof of the kind, and that he thought

the theory complete without it. I laughed at
him, and told him that without it the theory
would fall to the ground, and I warmly con-
gratulated him on the marvellous discovery.
We then arranged that the picture should be
etched or facsimiled, and placed as the frontis-
piece to Cyril's edition of the Sonnets; and for
three months we did nothing but go over each
poem line by line, till we had settled every difficulty of text or meaning. One unlucky day I
was in a print-shop in Holborn, when I saw
upon the counter some extremely beautiful
drawings in silver-point. I was so attracted by
them that I bought them; and the proprietor of
the place, a man called Rawlings, told me that
they were done by a young painter of the name
of Edward Merton, who was very clever, but
as poor as a church mouse. I went to see
Merton some days afterwards, having got his
address from the print-seller, and found a
pale, interesting young man, with a rather
common-looking wife—his model, as I subse-
quently learned. I told him how much I
admired his drawings, at which he seemed very
pleased, and I asked him if he would show me
some of his other work. As we were looking

over a portfolio, full of really very lovely
things,—foɪ Merton had a most delicate and
delightful touch,—I suddenly caught sight of a
drawing of the picture of Mr. W. H.   There
was no doubt whatever about it.   It was almost
a facsimile—the only difference being that the
two masks of Tragedy and Comedy were not
suspended from the marble table as they are in
the picture, but were lying on the floor at the
young man's feet.   'Where on earth did you
get that?' I said.   He grew rather confused, and
said—'Oh, that is nothing.   I did not know it
was in this portfolio.   It is not a thing of any
value.'   'It is what you did for Mr. Cyril
Graham,' exclaimed his wife; 'and if this gentleman wishes to buy it, let him have it.'   'For
Mr. Cyril Graham?' I repeated.   'Did you paint
the picture of Mr. W. H.?'   'I don't understand what you mean,' he answered, growing
very red.   Well, the whole thing was quite
dreadful.   The wife let it all out.   I gave her
five pounds when I was going away.   I can't
bear to think of it now; but of course I was
furious.   I went off at once to Cyril's chambers,.
waited there for three hours before he came in,.
with that horrid lie staring me in the face, and

told him I had discovered his forgery. He grew very pale, and said—'I did it purely for your sake. You would not be convinced in any other way. It does not affect the truth of the theory.' 'The truth of the theory!' I exclaimed; 'the less we talk about that the better. You never even believed in it yourself. If you had, you would not have committed a forgery to prove it.' High words passed between us; we had a fearful quarrel. I daresay I was unjust. The next morning he was dead.''

"Dead!" I cried.

"Yes; he shot himself with a revolver. Some of the blood splashed upon the frame of the picture, just where the name had been painted. By the time I arrived—his servant had sent for me at once—the police were already there. He had left a letter for me, evidently written in the greatest agitation and distress of mind.''

"What was in it?" I asked.

"Oh, that he believed absolutely in Willie Hughes; that the forgery of the picture had been done simply as a concession to me, and did not in the slightest degree invalidate the truth of the theory; and that in order to show me how firm and flawless his faith in the whole

thing was, he was going to offer his life as a
sacrifice to the secret of the Sonnets. It was a
foolish, mad letter. I remember he ended by
saying that he intrusted to me the Willie
Hughes theory, and that it was for me to present
it to the world, and to unlock the secret of
Shakespeare's heart.''

"It is a most tragic story," I cried; "but
why have you not carried out his wishes?"

Erskine shrugged his shoulders. "Because
it is a perfectly unsound theory from beginning
to end," he answered.

"My dear Erskine," I said, getting up from
my seat, "you are entirely wrong about the
whole matter. It is the only perfect key to
Shakespeare's Sonnets that has ever been made.
It is complete in every detail. I believe in
Willie Hughes."

"Don't say that," said Erskine, gravely; "I
believe there is something fatal about the idea,
and intellectually there is nothing to be said
for it. I have gone into the whole matter, and
I assure you the theory is entirely fallacious.
It is plausible up to a certain point. Then it
stops. For heaven's sake, my dear boy, don't

take up the subject of Willie Hughes. You will break your heart over it.''

''Erskine,'' I answered, ''it is your duty to give this theory to the world. If you will not do it, I will. By keeping it back you wrong the memory of Cyril Graham, the youngest and the most splendid of all the martyrs of literature. I entreat you to do him justice. He died for this thing,—don't let his death be in vain.''

Erskine looked at me in amazement. ''You are carried away by the sentiment of the whole story,'' he said. ''You forget that a thing is not necessarily true because a man dies for it. I was devoted to Cyril Graham. His death was a horrible blow to me. I did not recover it for years. I don't think I have ever recovered it. But Willie Hughes? There is nothing in the idea of Willie Hughes. No such person ever existed. As for bringing the whole thing before the world—the world thinks that Cyril Graham shot himself by accident. The only proof of his suicide was contained in the letter to me, and of this letter the public never heard anything. To the present day Lord Crediton thinks that the whole thing was accidental.''

''Cyril Graham sacrificed his life to a great

idea," I answered; "and if you will not tell of his martyrdom, tell at least of his faith."

"His faith," said Erskine, "was fixed in a thing that was false, in a thing that was unsound, in a thing that no Shakespearian scholar would accept for a moment. The theory would be laughed at. Don't make a fool of yourself, and don't follow a trail that leads nowhere. You start by assuming the existence of the very person whose existence is the thing to be proved. Besides, everybody knows that the Sonnets were addressed to Lord Pembroke. The matter is settled once for all."

"The matter is not settled!" I exclaimed. "I will take up the theory where Cyril Graham left it, and I will prove to the world that he was right."

"Silly boy!" said Erskine. "Go home; it is after two, and don't think about Willie Hughes any more. I am sorry I told you anything about it, and very sorry indeed that I should have converted you to a thing in which I don't believe."

"You have given me the key to the greatest mystery of modern literature," I answered; "and I shall not rest till I have made you recognise, till I have made everybody recognise, that Cyril Graham was the most subtle Shakespearian critic of our day.''

As I walked home through St. James's Park the dawn was just breaking over London. The white swans were lying asleep on the polished lake, and the gaunt Palace looked purple against the pale-green sky. I thought of Cyril Graham, and my eyes filled with tears.

## II.

It was past twelve o'clock when I awoke,
and the sun was streaming in through the
curtains of my room in long slanting beams
of dusty gold. I told my servant that I would
be at home to no one; and after I had had a
cup of chocolate and a *petit-pain,* I took down
from the bookshelf my copy of Shakespeare's
Sonnets, and began to go carefully through
them. Every poem seemed to me to corroborate Cyril Graham's theory. I felt as if I
had my hand upon Shakespeare's heart, and
was counting each separate throb and pulse
of passion. I thought of the wonderful boy-
actor, and saw his face in every line.

Two sonnets, I remember, struck me particularly: they were the 53rd and the 67th.
In the first of these, Shakespeare, compliment-
ing Willie Hughes on the versatility of his

acting, on his wide range of parts, a range
extending from Rosalind to Juliet, and from
Beatrice to Ophelia, says to him—

> " What is your substance, whereof are you made,
>     That millions of strange shadows on you tend?
>     Since every one hath, every one, one shade,
>     And you, but one, can every shadow lend "—

lines that would be unintelligible if they were
not addressed to an actor, for the word
"shadow" had in Shakespeare's day a technical meaning connected with the stage. "The
best in this kind, are but shadows," says
Theseus of the actors in the "Midsummer
Night's Dream," and there are many similar
allusions in the literature of the day. These
sonnets evidently belonged to the series in
which Shakespeare discusses the nature of the
actor's art, and of the strange and rare temperament that is essential to the perfect stage-
player. "How is it," says Shakespeare to
Willie Hughes, "that you have so many
personalities?" and then he goes on to point
out that his beauty is such that it seems to
realise every form and phase of fancy, to

embody each dream of the creative imagination
—an idea that is still further expanded in the
sonnet that immediately follows, where, beginning with the fine thought,

> " O, how much more doth beauty beauteous seem
>   By that sweet ornament which truth doth give! "

Shakespeare invites us to notice how the truth
of acting, the truth of visible presentation on
the stage, adds to the wonder of poetry, giving
life to its loveliness, and actual reality to its
ideal form.   And yet, in the 67th sonnet,
Shakespeare calls upon Willie Hughes to aban-
don the stage with its artificiality, its false
mimic life of painted face and unreal costume,
its immoral influences and suggestions, its
remoteness from the true world of noble action
and sincere utterance.

> " Ah! wherefore with infection should he live,
>   And with his presence grace impiety,
>   That sin by him advantage should achieve,
>   And lace itself with his society?
>   Why should false painting imitate his cheek
>   And steal dead seeming in his living hue?
>   Why should poor beauty indirectly seek
>   Roses of shadow, since his rose is true? "

It may seem strange that so great a dramatist
as Shakespeare, who realised his own perfection
as an artist and his humanity as a man on
the ideal plane of stage-writing and stage-
playing, should have written in these terms
about the theatre; but we must remember that
in Sonnets cx. and cxi. Shakespeare shows us
that he too was wearied of the world of
puppets, and full of shame at having made
himself "a motley to the view." The 111th
Sonnet is especially bitter:—

> "O, for my sake do you with Fortune chide
> The guilty goddess of my harmful deeds,
> That did not better for my life provide
> Than public means which public manners breeds.
> Thence comes it that my name receives a brand,
> And almost thence my nature is subdued
> To what it works in, like the dyer's hand:
> Pity me, then, and wish I were renewed "—

and there are many signs elsewhere of the
same feeling, signs familiar to all real students
of Shakespeare.

One point puzzled me immensely as I read
the Sonnets, and it was days before I struck
on the true interpretation, which indeed Cyril
Graham himself seems to have missed. I could

not understand how it was that Shakespeare
set so high a value on his young friend marrying.    He himself had married young, and the
result had been unhappiness, and it was not
likely that he would have asked Willie Hughes
to commit the same error.    The boy-player of
Rosalind had nothing to gain from marriage,
or from the passions of real life.    The early
sonnets, with their strange entreaties to have
children, seemed  to me a jarring note.    The
explanation of the mystery came on me quite
suddenly, and I found it in the curious dedication.    It will be remembered that the dedication runs as follows:—

"To · THE · ONLIE · BEGETTER · OF ·
THESE · INSUING · SONNETS ·
MR. W. H. · ALL · HAPPINESSE ·
AND · THAT · ETERNITIE ·
PROMISED · BY ·
OUR · EVER-LIVING · POET ·
WISHETH
THE · WELL-WISHING ·
ADVENTURER · IN ·
SETTING ·
FORTH.          T. T."

Some scholars have supposed that the word
"begetter" in this dedication means simply

the procurer of the Sonnets for Thomas Thorpe
the publisher; but this view is now generally
abandoned, and the highest authorities are
quite agreed that it is to be taken in the
sense of inspirer, the metaphor being drawn
from the analogy of physical life.. Now I saw
that the same metaphor was used by Shakespeare himself all through the poems, and this
set me on the right track. Finally I made my
great discovery. The marriage that Shakespeare proposes for Willie Hughes is the
"marriage with his Muse," an expression which
is definitely put forward in the 82nd Sonnet,
where, in the bitterness of his heart at the
defection of the boy-actor for whom he had
written his greatest parts, and whose beauty
had indeed suggested them, he opens his complaint by saying—

"I'll grant thou wert not married to my Muse."

The children he begs him to beget are no
children of flesh and blood, but more immortal
children of undying fame. The whole cycle of
the early sonnets is simply Shakespeare's invitation to Willie Hughes to go upon the stage and

become a player. How barren and profitless
a thing, he says, is this beauty of yours if it
be not used:

> " When forty winters shall besiege thy brow,
> And dig deep trenches in thy beauty's field,
> Thy youth's proud livery so gazed on now,
> Will be a tattered weed, of small worth held:
> Then being asked where all thy beauty lies,
> Where all the treasure of thy lusty days,
> To say within thine own deep-sunken eyes,
> Were an all-eating shame and thriftless praise."

You must create something in art; my verse
"is thine, and *born* of thee;" only listen to
me, and I will "*bring forth* eternal numbers
to outlive long date," and you shall people
with forms of your own image the imaginary
world of the stage. These children that you
beget, he continues, will not wither away, as
mortal children do, but you shall live in them
and in my plays: do but

> " Make thee another self, for love of me,
> That beauty still may live in thine or thee."

I collected all the passages that seemed to
me to corroborate this view, and they produced

a strong impression on me, and showed me how complete Cyril Graham's theory really was. I also saw that it was quite easy to separate those lines in which he speaks of the Sonnets themselves from those in which he speaks of his great dramatic work. This was a point that had been entirely over-looked by all critics up to Cyril Graham's day. And yet it was one of the most important points in the whole series of poems. To the Sonnets Shakespeare was more or less indifferent. He did not wish to rest his fame on them. They were to him his "slight Muse," as he calls them, and intended, as Meres tells us, for private circulation only among a few, a very few, friends. Upon the other hand he was extremely conscious of the high artistic value of his plays, and shows a noble self-reliance upon his dramatic genius. When he says to Willie Hughes:

> " But thy eternal summer shall not fade,
>   Nor lose possession of that fair thou owest;
>   Nor shall Death brag thou wander'st in his shade,
>   When in *eternal lines* to time thou growest;
>     So long as men can breathe or eyes can see,
>     So long lives this and this gives life to thee; "—

the expression "eternal lines" clearly alludes
to one of his plays that he was sending him
at the time, just as the concluding couplet
points to his confidence in the probability of
his plays being always acted.  In his address to
the Dramatic Muse (Sonnets c. and ci.), we find
the same feeling.

> " Where art thou, Muse, that thou forget'st so long
>   To speak of that which gives thee all thy might ?
>   Spends thou thy fury on some worthless song,
>   Darkening thy power to lend base subjects light ? "

he cries, and he then proceeds to reproach the
mistress of Tragedy and Comedy for her
"neglect of Truth in Beauty dyed," and says—

> " Because he needs no praise, wilt thou be dumb ?
>   Excuse not silence so; for 't lies in thee
>   To make him much outlive a gilded tomb,
>   And to be praised of ages yet to be.
>     Then do thy office, Muse; I teach thee how
>     To make him seem long hence as he shows now."

It is, however, perhaps in the 55th Sonnet that
Shakespeare gives to this idea its fullest expression.  To imagine that the "powerful rhyme"
of the second line refers to the sonnet itself, is to
entirely mistake Shakespeare's meaning.  It

seemed to me that it was extremely likely, from the general character of the sonnet, that a particular play was meant, and that the play was none other but "Romeo and Juliet."

> " Not marble, nor the gilded monuments
>   Of princes, shall outlive this powerful rhyme;
>   But you shall shine more bright in these contents
>   Than unswept stone besmeared with sluttish time.
>   When wasteful wars shall statues overturn,
>   And broils root out the work of masonry,
>   Not Mars his sword nor war's quick fire shall burn
>   The living record of your memory.
>   'Gainst death and all-oblivious enmity
>   Shall you pace forth; your praise shall still find room
>   Even in the eyes of all posterity
>   That wear this world out to the ending doom.
>     So, till the judgment that yourself arise,
>     You live in this and dwell in lover's eyes."

It was also extremely suggestive to note how here as elsewhere Shakespeare promised Willie Hughes immortality in a form that appealed to men's eyes—that is to say, in a spectacular form, in a play that is to be looked at.

For two weeks I worked hard at the Sonnets, hardly ever going out, and refusing all invitations. Every day I seemed to be discovering something new, and Willie Hughes became to me a kind of spiritual presence, an ever-dominant personality. I could almost fancy that I saw him standing in the shadow of my room, so well had Shakespeare drawn him, with his golden hair, his tender flower-like grace, his dreamy deep-sunken eyes, his delicate mobile limbs, and his white lily hands. His very name fascinated me. Willie Hughes! Willie Hughes! How musically it sounded! Yes; who else but he could have been the master-mistress of Shakespeare's passion,[1] the lord of his love to whom he was bound in vassalage,[2] the delicate minion of pleasure,[3] the rose of the whole world,[4] the herald of the spring,[5] decked in the proud livery of youth,[6] the lovely boy whom it was sweet music to hear,[7] and whose beauty was the very raiment of Shakespeare's heart,[8] as it was the keystone of his dramatic power? How bitter now seemed the whole tragedy of his desertion and shame!—shame that he made

---

[1] Sonnet xx. 2.
[2] Sonnet xxvi. 1.
[3] Sonnet cxxvi. 9.
[4] Sonnet cix. 14.
[5] Sonnet i. 10.
[6] Sonnet ii. 3.
[7] Sonnet viii. 1.
[8] Sonnet xxii. 6.

sweet and lovely [1] by the mere magic of his personality but that was none the less shame. Yet as Shakespeare forgave him, should not we forgive him also? I did not care to pry into the mystery of his sin.

His abandonment of Shakespeare's theatre was a different matter, and I investigated it at great length. Finally I came to the conclusion that Cyril Graham had been wrong in regarding the rival dramatist of the 80th Sonnet as Chapman. It was obviously Marlowe who was alluded to. At the time the Sonnets were written, such an expression as "the proud full sail of his great verse" could not have been used of Chapman's work, however applicable it might have been to the style of his later Jacobean plays. No: Marlowe was clearly the rival dramatist of whom Shakespeare spoke in such laudatory terms; and that

> "Affable familiar ghost
> Which nightly gulls him with intelligence,"

was the Mephistopheles of his Doctor Faustus. No doubt, Marlowe was fascinated by the beauty

---

[1] Sonnet xcv. 1.

and grace of the boy-actor, and lured him away from the Blackfriars' Theatre, that he might play the Gaveston of his "Edward II." That Shakespeare had the legal right to retain Willie Hughes in his own company is evident from Sonnet lxxxvii., where he says:—

> " Farewell! thou art too dear for my possessing,
>   And like enough thou know'st thy estimate:
>   The *charter of thy worth* gives thee releasing;
>   My *bonds* in thee are all determinate.
>   For how do I hold thee but by thy granting?
>   And for that riches where is my deserving?
>   The cause of this fair gift in me is wanting,
>   *And so my patent back again is swerving.*
>   Thyself thou gavest, thy own worth then not knowing,
>   Or me, to whom thou gavest it, else mistaking;
>   So thy great gift, upon misprision growing,
>   Comes not again, on better judgment making,
>     Thus I had thee, as a dream doth flatter,
>     In sleep a king, but waking no such matter."

But him whom he could not hold by love, he would not hold by force. Willie Hughes became a member of Lord Pembroke's company, and, perhaps in the open yard of the Red Bull Tavern, played the part of King Edward's delicate minion. On Marlowe's death, he seems to have returned to Shakespeare, who, whatever his fellow-partners  may have thought of the matter, was not slow to forgive the wilfulness and treachery of the young actor.

How well, too, had Shakespeare drawn the temperament of the stage-player! Willie Hughes was one of those

> "That do not do the thing they most do show,
> Who, moving others, are themselves as stone."

He could act love, but could not feel it, could mimic passion without realising it.

> "In many's looks the false heart's history
> Is writ in moods and frowns and wrinkles strange,"

but with Willie Hughes it was not so. "Heaven," says Shakespeare, in a sonnet of mad idolatry—

> "Heaven in thy creation did decree
> That in thy face sweet love should ever dwell;
> Whate'er thy thoughts or thy heart's workings be,
> Thy looks should nothing thence but sweetness tell."

In his "inconstant mind" and his "false heart," it was easy to recognise the insincerity and treachery that somehow seems inseparable from the artistic nature, as in his love of praise, that desire for immediate recognition that characterises all actors.  And yet, more fortunate in this than other actors, Willie Hughes was to know something of immortality.  Inseparably connected with Shakespeare's plays, he was to live in them.

> " Your name from hence immortal life shall have,
>   Though I, once gone, to all the world must die;
>   The earth can yield me but a common grave,
>   When you entombed in men's eyes shall lie.
>   Your monument shall be my gentle verse,
>   Which eyes not yet created shall o'er-read,
>   And tongues to be your being shall rehearse
>   When all the breathers of this world are dead."

There were endless allusions, also, to Willie Hughes's power over his audience, — the "gazers," as Shakespeare calls them; but perhaps the most perfect description of his wonderful mastery over dramatic art was in "The Lover's Complaint," where Shakespeare says of him:—

> " In him a plentitude of subtle matter,
>   Applied to cautels, all strange forms receives,
>   Of burning blushes, or of weeping water,
>   Or swooning paleness; and he takes and leaves,
>   In either's aptness, as it best deceives,
>   To blush at speeches rank, to weep at woes,
>   Or to turn white and swoon at tragic shows,
>   .   .   .   .   .   .   .   .   .

So on the tip of his subduing tongue,
All kind of arguments and questions deep,
All replication prompt and reason strong,
For his advantage still did wake and sleep,
To make the weeper laugh, the laugher weep.
  He had the dialect and the different skill,
  Catching all passions in his craft of will."

Once I thought that I had really found Willie Hughes in Elizabethan literature. In a wonderfully graphic account of the last days of the great Earl of Essex, his chaplain, Thomas Knell, tells us that the night before the Earl died, "he called William Hewes, which was his musician, to play upon the virginals and to sing. 'Play,' said he, 'my song, Will Hews, and I will sing it myself.' So he did most joyfully, not as the howling swan, which, still looking down, waileth her end, but as a sweet lark, lifting up his hands and casting up his eyes to his God, with this mounted the crystal skies, and reached with his unwearied tongue the top of highest heavens." Surely the boy who played on the virginals to the dying father of Sidney's Stella was none other but the Will Hews to whom Shakespeare dedicated the Sonnets, and whom he tells us was himself sweet "music to hear."

Yet Lord Essex died in 1576, when Shakespeare himself was but twelve years of age. It was impossible that his musician could have been the Mr. W. H. of the Sonnets. Perhaps Shakespeare's young friend was the son of the player upon the virginals? It was at least something to have discovered that Will Hews was an Elizabethan name. Indeed the name Hews seemed to have been closely connected with music and the stage. The first English actress was the lovely Margaret Hews, whom Prince Rupert so madly loved. What more probable than that between her and Lord Essex's musician had come the boy-actor of Shakespeare's plays? But the proofs, the links—where were they? Alas! I could not find them. It seemed to me that I was always on the brink of absolute verification, but that I could never really attain to it.

From Willie Hughes's life I soon passed to thoughts of his death. I used to wonder what had been his end.

Perhaps he had been one of those English actors who in 1604 went across sea to Germany and played before the great Duke Henry Julius of Brunswick, himself a dramatist of no mean order, and at the Court of that strange Elector of Brandenburg, who was so enamoured of beauty that he was said to have bought for his weight in amber the young son of a travelling Greek merchant, and to have given pageants in honour of his slave all through that dreadful famine year of 1606-7, when the people died of hunger in the very streets of the town, and for the space of seven months there was no rain. We know at any rate that "Romeo and Juliet" was brought out at Dresden in 1613, along with "Hamlet" and "King Lear," and it was surely to none other than Willie Hughes that in 1615 the death-mask of Shakespeare was brought by the hand of one of the suite of the English ambassador, pale token of the passing away of the great poet who had so dearly loved him. Indeed there would have been something peculiarly fitting in the idea that the boy-actor, whose beauty had been so vital an element in the realism and romance of Shakespeare's art, should have been the first to have brought to Germany the seed of the new culture, and was in his way the precursor of that *Aufklarung* or Illumination of the eighteenth century, that splendid movement which, though begun by Lessing and Herder, and brought to its full and

perfect issue by Goethe, was in no small
part helped on by another actor—Friedrich
Schroeder—who awoke the popular consciousness, and by means of the feigned passions and
mimetic methods of the stage showed the inti-
mate, the vital, connection between life and literature.  If this was so,—and there was certainly
no evidence against it,—it was not improbable
that Willie Hughes was one of those English
comedians (*mimæ quidam ex Britannia*, as the
old chronicle calls them), who were slain at
Nuremberg in a sudden uprising of the people,
and were secretly buried in a little vineyard
outside the city by some young men "who had
found pleasure in their performances, and of
whom some had sought to be instructed in the
mysteries of the new art."  Certainly no more
fitting place could there be for him to whom
Shakespeare said, "thou art all my art," than
this little vineyard outside the city walls.  For
was it not from the sorrows of Dionysos that
Tragedy sprang? Was not the light laughter of
Comedy, with its careless merriment and quick
replies, first heard on the lips of the Sicilian
vine-dressers? Nay, did not the purple and red
stain of the wine-froth on face and limbs give

the first suggestion of the charm and fascination of disguise—the desire for self-concealment, the sense of the value of objectivity thus showing itself in the rude beginnings of the art? At any rate, wherever he lay—whether in the little vineyard at the gate of the Gothic town, or in some dim London churchyard amidst the roar and bustle of our great city—no gorgeous monument marked his resting-place. His true tomb, as Shakespeare saw, was the poet's verse, his true monument the permanence of the drama. So had it been with others whose beauty had given a new creative impulse to their age. The ivory body of the Bithynian slave rots in the green ooze of the Nile, and on the yellow hills of the Cerameicus is strewn the dust of the young Athenian; but Antinous lives in sculpture, and Charmides in philosophy.

## III.

After three weeks had elapsed, I determined
to make a strong appeal to Erskine to do justice
to the memory of Cyril Graham, and to give to
the world his marvellous interpretation of the
Sonnets—the only interpretation that thoroughly explained the problem. I have not any copy
of my letter, I regret to say, nor have I been able
to lay my hand upon the original; but I remember that I went over the whole ground, and
covered sheets of paper with passionate reitera-
tion of the arguments and proofs that my study
had suggested to me. It seemed to me that I
was not merely restoring Cyril Graham to his
proper place in literary history, but rescuing
the honour of Shakespeare himself from the
tedious memory of a commonplace intrigue. I
put into the letter all my enthusiasm. I put
into the letter all my faith.

No sooner, in fact, had I sent it off than a
curious reaction came over me. It seemed to

me that I had given away my capacity for belief in the Willie Hughes theory of the Sonnets, that something had gone out of me, as it were, and that I was perfectly indifferent to the whole subject. What was it that had happened? It is difficult to say. Perhaps, by finding perfect expression for a passion, I had exhausted the passion itself. Emotional forces, like the forces of physical life, have their positive limitations. Perhaps the mere effort to convert any one to a theory involves some form of renunciation of the power of credence. Perhaps I was simply tired of the whole thing, and, my enthusiasm having burnt out, my reason was left to its own unimpassioned judgment. However, it came about, and I cannot pretend to explain it, there was no doubt that Willie Hughes suddenly became to me a mere myth, an idle dream, the boyish fancy of a young man who, like most ardent spirits, was more anxious to convince others than to be himself convinced.

As I had said some very unjust and bitter things to Erskine in my letter, I determined to go and see him at once, and to make my apologies to him for my behaviour. Accordingly, the next morning I drove down to

Birdcage Walk, and found Erskine sitting in his library, with the forged picture of Willie Hughes in front of him.

"My dear Erskine!" I cried, "I have come to apologise to you."

"To apologise to me?" he said. "What for?"

"For my letter," I answered.

"You have nothing to regret in your letter," he said. "On the contrary, you have done me the greatest service in your power. You have shown me that Cycil Graham's theory is perfectly sound."

"You don't mean to say that you believe in Willie Hughes?" I exclaimed.

"Why not?" he rejoined. "You have proved the thing to me. Do you think I cannot estimate the value of evidence?"

"But there is no evidence at all," I groaned, sinking into a chair. "When I wrote to you I was under the influence of a perfectly silly enthusiasm. I had been touched by the story of Cyril Graham's death, fascinated by his romantic theory, enthralled by the wonder and novelty of the whole idea. I see now that the theory is based on a delusion. The only evidence for the existence of Willie Hughes is that picture in front of you, and the picture is a forgery. Don't be carried away by mere sentiment in this matter. Whatever romance may have to say about the Willie Hughes theory, reason is dead against it.''

''I don't understand you,'' said Erskine, looking at me in amazement. ''Why, you yourself have convinced me by your letter that Willie Hughes is an absolute reality. Why have you changed your mind? Or is all that you have been saying to me merely a joke?''

''I cannot explain it to you,'' I rejoined, ''but I see now that there is really nothing to be said in favour of Cyril Graham's interpretation. The Sonnets are addressed to Lord Pembroke. For heaven's sake don't waste your time in a foolish attempt to discover a young Elizabethan actor who never existed, and to make a phantom puppet the centre of the great cycle of Shakespeare's Sonnets.''

''I see that you don't understand the theory,'' he replied.

''My dear Erskine,'' I cried, ''not understand it! Why, I feel as if I had invented it. Surely my letter shows you that I not merely went into the whole matter, but that I contributed proofs of every kind. The one flaw in the theory is that it presupposes the existence of the person whose existence is the subject of dispute. If we grant that there was in Shakespeare's company a young actor of the name of Willie Hughes, it is not difficult to make him the object of the Sonnets. But as we know that there was no actor of this name in the company of the Globe Theatre, it is idle to pursue the investigation further.''

''But that is exactly what we don't know,'' said Erskine. ''It is quite true that his name does not occur in the list given in the first folio; but, as Cyril pointed out, that is rather a proof in favour of the existence of Willie Hughes than against it, if we remember his treacherous desertion of Shakespeare for a rival dramatist.''

We argued the matter over for hours, but nothing that I could say could make Erskine surrender his faith in Cyril Graham's interpretation. He told me that he intended to devote his life to proving the theory, and that he was determined to do justice to Cyril Graham's memory. I entreated him, laughed at him, begged of him, but it was of no use.

Finally we parted, not exactly in anger, but certainly with a shadow between us. He thought me shallow, I thought him foolish. When I called on him again, his servant told me that he had gone to Germany.

Two years afterwards, as I was going into my club, the hall-porter handed me a letter with a foreign postmark. It was from Erskine, and written at the Hotel d'Angleterre, Cannes. When I had read it I was filled with horror, though I did not quite believe that he would be so mad as to carry his resolve into execution. The gist of the letter was that he had tried in every way to verify the Willie Hughes theory, and had failed, and that as Cyril Graham had given his life for this theory, he himself had determined to give his own life also to the same cause. The concluding words of the letter were these: "I still believe in Willie Hughes; and by the time you receive this, I shall have died by my own hand for Willie Hughes's sake: for his sake, and for the sake of Cyril Graham, whom I drove to his death by my shallow scepticism and ignorant lack of faith. The truth was once revealed to you and you rejected it. It comes to you now stained with the blood of two lives,—do not turn away from it.''

It was a horrible moment. I felt sick with misery, and yet I could not believe it. To die for one's theological beliefs is the worst use a man can make of his life, but to die for a literary theory! It seemed impossible.

I looked at the date. The letter was a week old. Some unfortunate chance had prevented my going to the club for several days, or I might have got it in time to save him. Perhaps it was not too late. I drove off to my rooms, packed up my things, and started by the night-mail from Charing Cross. The journey was intolerable. I thought I would never arrive.

As soon as I did I drove to the Hotel d'Angle-terre. They told me that Erskine had been buried two days before, in the English cemetery. There was something horribly grotesque about the whole tragedy. I said all kinds of wild things, and the people in the hall looked curiously at me.

Suddenly Lady Erskine, in deep mourning, passed across the vestibule. When she saw me she came up to me, murmured something about her poor son, and burst into tears. I led her into her sitting-room. An elderly gentleman was there waiting for her. It was the English doctor.

We talked a great deal about Erskine, but I said nothing about his motive for committing suicide. It was evident that he had not told his mother anything about the reason that had driven him to so fatal, so mad an act. Finally Lady Erskine rose and said, ''George left you something as a memento. It was a thing he prized very much. I will get it for you.''

As soon as she had left the room I turned to the doctor and said, ''What a dreadful shock it must have been to Lady Erskine! I wonder that she bears it as well as she does.''

''Oh, she knew for months past that it was coming,'' he answered.

''Knew it for months past!'' I cried. ''But why didn't she stop him? Why didn't she have him watched? He must have been mad.''

The doctor stared at me. ''I don't know what you mean,'' he said.

''Well,'' I cried, ''if a mother knows that her son is going to commit suicide——''

''Suicide!'' he answered. ''Poor Erskine did not commit suicide. He died of consumption.

He came here to die. The moment I saw him I knew that there was no hope. One lung was almost gone, and the other was very much affected. Three days before he died he asked me was there any hope. I told him frankly that there was none, and that he had only a few days to live. He wrote some letters, and was quite resigned, retaining his senses to the last.''

At that moment Lady Erskine entered the room with the fatal picture of Willie Hughes in her hand. ''When George was dying he begged me to give you this,'' she said. As I took it from her, her tears fell on my hand.

The picture hangs now in my library, where it is very much admired by my artistic friends. They have decided that it is not a Clouet, but an Ouvry. I have never cared to tell them its true history. But sometimes, when I look at it, I think that there is really a great deal to be said for the Willie Hughes theory of Shakespeare's Sonnets.

1889.

# Impressions of America,

with an Introduction by

## Stuart Mason.

# INTRODUCTION.

Oscar Wilde visited America in the year 1882. Interest in the Æsthetic School, of which he was already the acknowledged master, had sometime previously spread to the United States, and it is said that the production of the Gilbert and Sullivan opera, "Patience," * in which he and his disciples were held up to ridicule, determined him to pay a visit to the States to give some lectures explaining what he meant by Æstheticism, hoping thereby to interest, and possibly to instruct and elevate our transatlantic cousins.

He set sail on board the "Arizona" on Saturday, December 24th, 1881, arriving in New York early in the following year. On landing he was bombarded by journalists eager to interview the distinguished stranger. "Punch," in its issue

---

* First produced at the Opera Comique, April 23rd, 1881. Wilde was burlesqued as Reginald Bunthorne, a Fleshly Poet.

of January 14th, in a happy vein, parodied these interviewers, the most amusing passage in which referred to "His Glorious Past," wherein Wilde was made to say, "Precisely—I took the Newdigate. Oh! no doubt, every year some man gets the Newdigate; but not every year does Newdigate get an Oscar."

At Omaha, where, under the auspices of the Social Art Club, Wilde delivered a lecture on "Decorative Art," he describes his impressions of many American houses as being "illy designed, decorated shabbily, and in bad taste, filled with furniture that was not honestly made, and was out of character." This statement gave rise to the following verses:—

What a shame and what a pity,
In the streets of London City
  Mr. Wilde is seen no more.
Far from Piccadilly banished,
He to Omaha has vanished.
  Horrid place, which swells ignore.

On his back a coat he beareth,
Such as Sir John Bennet weareth,

Made of velvet—strange array!
Legs Apollo might have sighed for,
Or great Hercules have died for,
    His knee breeches now display.


Waving sunflower and lily,
He calls all the houses "illy
    Decorated and designed."
For of taste they've not a tittle;
They may chew and they may whittle;
    But they're all born colour-blind!


His lectures dealt almost exclusively with the
subjects of Art and Dress Reform.  In the course
of one lecture he remarked that the most impressive room he had yet entered in America was the
one in Camden Town where he met Walt Whitman.  It contained plenty of fresh air and sun-
light.  On the table was a simple cruse of water.
This led to a parody, in the style of Whitman,
describing an imaginary interview between the
two poets, which appeared in "The Century" a
few months later.  Wilde is called Narcissus and
Whitman Paumanokides.

Paumanokides :—

> Who may this be?
>
> This young man clad unusually with loose
>   locks, languorous, glidingly toward me
>   advancing,
>
> Toward the ceiling of my chamber his orbic
>   and expressive eyeballs uprolling,

and so on, to which Narcissus replies,

> O clarion, from whose brazen throat,
>   Strange sounds across the seas are blown,
> Where England, girt as with a moat,
>   A strong sea-lion sits alone!

Of the lectures which he delivered in America
only one has been preserved, namely that on the
English Renaissance. This was his first lecture,
and it was delivered in New York on January
9th, 1882. According to a contemporary account
in the "New York Herald" a distinguished and
crowded audience assembled in Chickering Hall
that evening to listen to one who "was well
worth seeing, his short breeches and silk stock-
ings showing to even better advantage upon the

stage than in the gilded drawing-rooms, where the young Apostle has heretofore been seen in New York." *

On leaving the States in the "fall" of the year Wilde proceeded to Canada and thence to Nova Scotia, arriving in Halifax in the second week of October. Of his visit there we have no record except an amusing interview described in a local paper a few days later. He was dressed in a velvet jacket with an ordinary linen collar and necktie and he wore trousers. "Mr. Wilde," the interviewer states, "was communicative and genial; he said he found Canada pleasant, but in answer to a question as to whether European or American women were the more beautiful, he dexterously evaded his querist."

As regards poetry he expressed his opinion

---

* Wilde repeated this lecture throughout the States during his tour. At Rochester, on February 7th, he met with a most disorderly reception on the part of the College Students. Two days later Mr. Joaquin Miller, of St. Louis, wrote to Wilde saying that he had "read with shame about the behaviour of those ruffians." To this Wilde replied, "I thank you for your chivalrous and courteous letter," and in the course of his letter makes a more special attack on that critic whom he terms "the itinerant libeller of New England."

that Poe was the greatest American poet, and
that Walt Whitman, if not a poet, was a man
who sounded a strong note, perhaps neither
prose nor poetry, but something of his own that
was "grand, original and unique."

During his tour in America Wilde "happened
to find" himself (as he has himself described
it), in Louisville, Kentucky. The subject he had
selected to speak on was the Mission of Art in
the Nineteenth Century. In the course of his
lecture he had occasion to quote Keats' Sonnet
on Blue "as an example of the poet's delicate
sense of colour-harmonies." After the lecture
there came round to see him "a lady of middle
age, with a sweet gentle manner and most
musical voice," who introduced herself as Mrs.
Speed, the daughter of George Keats, and she
invited the lecturer to come and examine the
Keats manuscripts in her possession.

Some months afterwards when lecturing in
California he received a letter from this lady
asking him to accept the original manuscript of
the sonnet which he had quoted.

Mention must be made of Wilde's first play,
a drama in blank verse entitled "Vera, or the
Nihilists." It had been arranged that, before

his departure for America, this play should be
performed at the Adelphi Theatre, London, with
Mrs. Bernard Beere as the heroine, on Saturday,
December 17th, 1881, but a few weeks before the
date fixed for the first performance, the author
decided to postpone the production "owing to
the state of political feeling in England."

On his return to England in 1883 Wilde
started on a lecturing tour, the first being to the
Art Students of the Royal Academy at their
Club in Golden Square on June 30th.  Ten days
later he spoke at Prince's Hall on his "Personal
Impressions of America," and on subsequent
occasions at Margate, Ramsgate and Southampton.  On Monday, July 30th, he lectured at
Southport and on the following Thursday he
went to Liverpool to welcome Mrs. Langtry on
her return from America, and the same afternoon he left on his second visit to the States in
order to superintend the rehearsals of "Vera,"
which it had been arranged to produce at the
Union Square Theatre, New York, on August
20th following.  The piece was not a success—
it was, indeed, the only failure Wilde had.  However, his next play, which he called his "Opus
Secundum," also a blank verse tragedy, had a

successful run in America in 1891. This was "The Duchess of Padua," played by Lawrence Barrett, under the title of "Guido Ferranti." This has not been seen in England, nor is it even possible for Wilde's admirers to read this early offspring of his pen, for only twenty copies were printed for acting purposes in America and of these but one is known to be in existence, in this country at least.

An authorised German translation was made by Max Meyerfeld and the first performance took place at the German Theatre in Hamburg about a year ago. An English version is advertised from a piratical publisher in Paris but it is only a translation from the German back into English.

Towards the end of September 1883 Oscar Wilde returned to England and immediately began "an all round lecturing tour," his first visit being to Wandsworth Town Hall on Monday, September 24th, when he delivered to an enthusiastic audience a lecture on his "Impressions of America," which is contained in the following pages. He was dressed, a London paper of the times states, "in ordinary evening costume, and carried an orange-coloured silk handkerchief in his breast. He spoke with great fluency, in a voice now and then singularly musical, and only once or twice made a scarcely perceptible reference to notes.'' The lecture was under the auspices of a local Literary Society, and the principal residents of the district turned out ''en masse.'' The Chairman, the Rev. John Park, in introducing the lecturer, said there were two reasons why he was glad to welcome him, and he thought his own feelings would be shared by the audience. They must all plead guilty to a feeling of curiosity, he hoped a laudable one, to see and hear Mr. Wilde for his own sake, and they were also glad to hear about America—a country which many might regard as a kind of Elysium.

On March 5th in the following year Wilde lectured at the Crystal Palace on his American experiences, and on April 26th he ''preached his Gospel in the East-end,'' when it is recorded that his audience was not only delighted with his humour, but was ''surprised at the excellent good sense he talked.'' His subject was a plea in favour of ''art for schools,'' and many of his remarks about the English system of elementary education—with its insistence on ''the population of places that no one ever wants to go to," and its "familiarity with the lives of persons who probably never existed"—were said to be quite worthy of Ruskin. A contemporary account adds that Wilde "showed himself a pupil of Mr. Ruskin's, too, in insisting on the importance of every child being taught some handicraft, and in looking forward to the time when a boy would rather look at a bird or even draw it than throw "his customary stone!"

The British "gamin" has not made much progress in this respect during the last twenty years!

His lectures on "Dress," with the newspaper correspondence which they evoked, including some of Oscar Wilde's replies in his most characteristic vein, must be reserved for a future volume.

*Oxford, January 1906.*

# IMPRESSIONS OF AMERICA.

I fear I cannot picture America as altogether
an Elysium—perhaps, from the ordinary stand-
point I know but little about the country. I
cannot give its latitude or longitude; I cannot
compute the value of its dry goods, and I have
no very close acquaintance with its politics.
These are matters which may not interest you,
and they certainly are not interesting to me.

The first thing that struck me on landing in
America was that if the Americans are not the
most well-dressed people in the world, they are
the most comfortably dressed. Men are seen
there with the dreadful chimney-pot hat, but
there are very few hatless men; men wear the
shocking swallow-tail coat, but few are to be seen
with no coat at all. There is an air of comfort
in the appearance of the people which is a
marked contrast to that seen in this country,
where, too often, people are seen in close con-
tact with rags.

The next thing particularly noticeable is that everybody seems in a hurry to catch a train. This is a state of things which is not favourable to poetry or romance. Had Romeo or Juliet been in a constant state of anxiety about trains, or had their minds been agitated by the question of return-tickets, Shakespeare could not have given us those lovely balcony scenes which are so full of poetry and pathos.

America is the noisiest country that ever existed. One is waked up in the morning, not by the singing of the nightingale, but by the steam whistle. It is surprising that the sound practical sense of the Americans does not reduce this intolerable noise. All Art depends upon exquisite and delicate sensibility, and such continual turmoil must ultimately be destructive of the musical faculty.

There is not so much beauty to be found in American cities as in Oxford, Cambridge, Salisbury or Winchester, where are lovely relics of a beautiful age; but still there is a good deal of beauty to be seen in them now and then, but only where the American has not attempted to create it. Where the Americans have attempted to produce beauty they have signally failed. A remarkable characteristic of the Americans is the manner in which they have applied science to modern life.

This is apparent in the most cursory stroll through New York. In England an inventor is regarded almost as a crazy man, and in too many instances invention ends in disappointment and poverty. In America an inventor is honoured, help is forthcoming, and the exercise of ingenuity, the application of science to the work of man, is there the shortest road to wealth. There is no country in the world where machinery is so lovely as in America.

I have always wished to believe that the line of strength and the line of beauty are one. That wish was realised when I contemplated American machinery. It was not until I had seen the water-works at Chicago that I realised the wonders of machinery; the rise and fall of the steel rods, the symmetrical motion of the great wheels is the most beautifully rhythmic thing I have ever seen.* One is impressed in

---

* In a poem published in an American magazine on February 15th, 1882, Wilde wrote

"And in the throbbing engine room
Leap the long rods of polished steel."

America, but not favourably impressed, by the inordinate size of everything. The country seems to try to bully one into a belief in its power by its impressive bigness.

I was disappointed with Niagara—most people must be disappointed with Niagara. Every American bride is taken there, and the sight of the stupendous waterfall must be one of the earliest, if not the keenest, disappointments in American married life. One sees it under bad conditions, very far away, the point of view not showing the splendour of the water. To appreciate it really one has to see it from underneath the fall, and to do that it is necessary to be dressed in a yellow oil-skin, which is as ugly as a mackintosh—and I hope none of you ever wears one. It is a consolation to know, however, that such an artist as Madame Bernhardt has not only worn that yellow, ugly dress, but has been photographed in it.

Perhaps the most beautiful part of America is the West, to reach which, however, involves a journey by rail of six days, racing along tied to an ugly tin-kettle of a steam engine. I found but poor consolation for this journey in the fact that the boys who infest the cars and sell everything that one can eat—or should not eat—were selling editions of my poems vilely printed on a kind of grey blotting paper, for the low price of ten cents.* Calling these boys on one side I told them that though poets like to be popular they desire to be paid, and selling editions of my poems without giving me a profit is dealing a blow at literature which must have a disastrous effect on poetical aspirants. The invariable reply that they made was that they themselves made a profit out of the transaction and that was all they cared about.

It is a popular superstition that in America a visitor is invariably addressed as "Stranger." I was never once addressed as "Stranger." When I went to Texas I was called "Captain"; when I got to the centre of the country I was addressed as "Colonel," and, on arriving at the borders of Mexico, as "General." On the whole, however, "Sir," the old English method of addressing people is the most common.

---

*Poems by Oscar Wilde. Also his Lecture on the English Renaissance.* The Seaside Library, Vol. lviii. No. 1183, January 19th, 1882. 4to. Pp. 32. New York: George Munro, Publisher.

A copy of this edition was sold by auction in New York last year for eight dollars.

It is, perhaps, worth while to note that what many people call Americanisms are really old English expressions which have lingered in our colonies while they have been lost in our own country. Many people imagine that the term "I guess," which is so common in America, is purely an American expression, but it was used by John Locke in his work on "The Understanding," just as we now use "I think." *

It is in the colonies, and not in the mother country, that the old life of the country really exists. If one wants to realise what English Puritanism is—not at its worst (when it is very bad), but at its best, and then it is not very good —I do not think one can find much of it in England, but much can be found about Boston and Massachusetts. We have got rid of it. America still preserves it, to be, I hope, a short-lived curiosity.

San Francisco is a really beautiful city.

---

* See *An Essay concerning Human Understanding*, IV. xii. 10.

A still more striking instance of the use of this expression is to be found in the same writer's *Thoughts concerning Education*, s. 28, where he says:—" Once in four and twenty hours, I think, is enough; and nobody, *I guess*, will think it too much."

China Town, peopled by Chinese labourers, is the most artistic town I have ever come across. The people—strange, melancholy Orientals, whom many people would call common, and they are certainly very poor—have determined that they will have nothing about them that is not beautiful. In the Chinese restaurant, where these navvies meet to have supper in the evening, I found them drinking tea out of china cups as delicate as the petals of a rose-leaf, whereas at the gaudy hotels I was supplied with a delf cup an inch and a half thick. When the Chinese bill was presented it was made out on rice paper, the account being done in Indian ink as fantastically as if an artist had been etching little birds on a fan.

Salt Lake City contains only two buildings of note, the chief being the Tabernacle, which is in the shape of a soup-kettle. It is decorated by the only native artist, and he has treated religious subjects in the native spirit of the early Florentine painters, representing people of our own day in the dress of the period side by side with people of Biblical history who are clothed in some romantic costume.

The building next in importance is called the

Amelia Palace, in honour of one of Brigham Young's wives. When he died the present president of the Mormons stood up in the Tabernacle and said that it had been revealed to him that he was to have the Amelia Palace, and that on this subject there were to be no more revelations of any kind!

From Salt Lake City one travels over the great plains of Colorado, and up the Rocky Mountains, on the top of which is Leadville, the richest city in the world. It has also got the reputation of being the roughest, and every man carries a revolver. I was told that if I went there they would be sure to shoot me or my travelling manager. I wrote and told them that nothing that they could do to my travelling manager would intimidate me. They are miners—men working in metals, so I lectured to them on the Ethics of Art. I read them passages from the autobiography of Benvenuto Cellini and they seemed much delighted. I was reproved by my hearers for not having brought him with me. I explained that he had been dead for some little time which elicited the enquiry "Who shot him"? They afterwards took me to a dancing saloon where I saw the only rational method of art criticism I have ever come across.   Over the piano was printed a notice:—

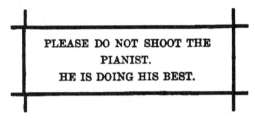

> PLEASE DO NOT SHOOT THE
> PIANIST.
> HE IS DOING HIS BEST.

The mortality among pianists in that place is marvellous.   Then they asked me to supper, and having accepted, I had to descend a mine in a rickety bucket in which it was impossible to be graceful.   Having got into the heart of the mountain I had supper, the first course being whisky, the second whisky and the third whisky.

I went to the Theatre to lecture and I was informed that just before I went there two men had been seized for committing a murder, and in that theatre they had been brought on to the stage at eight o'clock in the evening, and then and there tried and executed before a crowded audience.   But I found these miners very charming and not at all rough.

Among the more elderly inhabitants of the

South I found a melancholy tendency to date every event of importance by the late war. "How beautiful the moon is to-night," I once remarked to a gentleman who was standing next to me. "Yes," was his reply, "but you should have seen it before the war."

So infinitesimal did I find the knowledge of Art, west of the Rocky Mountains, that an art patron—one who in his day had been a miner—actually sued the railroad company for damages because the plaster cast of Venus of Milo, which he had imported from Paris, had been delivered minus the arms. And, what is more surprising still, he gained his case and the damages.

Pennsylvania, with its rocky gorges and woodland scenery, reminded me of Switzerland.. The prairie reminded me of a piece of blotting paper.

The Spanish and French have left behind them memorials in the beauty of their names. All the cities that have beautiful names derive them from the Spanish or the French. The English people give intensely ugly names to places. One place had such an ugly name that I refused to lecture there. It was called Grigsville. Supposing I had founded a School of

Art there—fancy "Early Grigsville." Imagine a School of Art teaching "Grigsville Renais-sance."

As for slang I did not hear much of it, though a young lady who had changed her clothes after an afternoon dance did say that "after the heel kick she shifted her day goods."

American youths are pale and precocious, or sallow and supercilious, but American girls are pretty and charming—little oases of pretty un-reasonableness in a vast desert of practical com-mon-sense.

Every American girl is entitled to have twelve young men devoted to her. They remain her slaves and she rules them with charming non-chalance.

The men are entirely given to business; they have, as they say, their brains in front of their heads. They are also exceedingly acceptive of new ideas. Their education is practical. We base the education of children entirely on books, but we must give a child a mind before we can instruct the mind. Children have a natural an-tipathy to books—handicraft should be the basis of education. Boys and girls should be taught to use their hands to make something, and they would be less apt to destroy and be mischievous.

In going to America one learns that poverty is not a necessary accompaniment to civilisation. There at any rate is a country that has no trappings, no pageants and no gorgeous ceremonies. I saw only two processions—one was the Fire Brigade preceded by the Police, the other was the Police preceded by the Fire Brigade.

Every man when he gets to the age of twenty-one is allowed to vote, and thereby immediately acquires his political education. The Americans are the best politically educated people in the world. It is well worth one's while to go to a country which can teach us the beauty of the word *FREEDOM* and the value of the thing *LIBERTY*.

# OSCAR WILDE IN AMERICA.

An interesting account of Oscar Wilde, at the time of his American tour, was given in the *Lady's Pictorial* a few weeks after his arrival in New York, the city which he described as "one huge Whiteley's shop."

He was interviewed in a room which was intensely warm and the sofa on which the poet reclined was drawn up to the fire. An immense wolf rug, bordered with scarlet, was thrown over it and half-encircled his graceful form in its warm embrace. Wilde was wearied. In a languid, half enervated manner he gently sipped hot chocolate from a cup by his side. Occasionally he inhaled a long, deep whiff from a smouldering cigarette held lightly in his white and shapely hand.

He was attired in a smoking suit of dark

brown velvet faced with lapels of red quilted silk. The ends of a long dark necktie floated over the facing like sea-weed on foam tinged by the dying sun. Dark brown nether garments, striped with red up the seam, and patent leather shoes with light cloth uppers completed the rest of the poet's costume.

His favourite colour is said to have been something between brown and green, a tint "that never was on sea or sky," and he had a complete suit made of it. A white walking-stick which he was in the habit of carrying was presented to him at the Acropolis and was said to have been cut from the olive groves of the Academia. Only in the evening was he wont to don knee breeches, "but evening and morning alike," adds his interviewer, "find him neither more nor less than a man, and always a perfect gentleman."

Long masses of dark brown hair, parted in the middle, fell in odd curves of beauty over his broad shoulders. He wore neither beard nor moustache. The full, rather sensuous lips, now pressed close together with momentary tension, now parted in kindly smile, showed to perfection the nobility of his countenance.

A Grecian nose and a well-tinged flush of

health on the poet's face added all that was
required to make it a truly remarkable one. The
eyes were large, dark* and ever-changing in
expression. He was a charming companion who
could tell racy stories and repeat *bon mots* of
those whom society delighted to honour, and at
the same time could cap quotations from Greek
authors.

---

* A French writer, M. Joseph-Renaud, recently
described Wilde's eyes as being *blue*, while Lord Alfred
Douglas affirms that they were *green*.

---

The two poems *Le Jardin* and *La Mer* appeared
originally in the first number of *Our Continent*, an
American Magazine, in February, 1882. They have not
been reprinted or included in any edition of the collected
poems.

## Date Due

| | | | |
|---|---|---|---|
| | | | |
| | | | |
| | | | |
| | | | |
| | | | |
| | | | |
| | | | |
| | | | |
| | | | |
| | | | |
| | | | |
| | | | |
| | | | |
| | | | |
| | | | |
| | | | |
| | | | |

CPSIA information can be obtained at www.ICGtesting.com
Printed in the USA
BVOW06*0219031215

429249BV00009B/45/P